BURGER
NIGHT

KATE McMILLAN

PHOTOGRAPHS BY ERIN KUNKEL

weldon**owen**

CONTENTS

INTRODUCTION 7

ANATOMY OF A BURGER 8

BURGER PRIMER 11

ESSENTIALS
Quick Dill Pickles 18

Ketchup 20

Basic Yellow Mustard 21

Basic Aioli 24

Vanilla Milkshakes & Malts 25

Sautéed Mushrooms 27

Onions Three Ways 28

BURGERS

 MEAT & POULTRY
Caprese Burgers 32

Gorgonzola-Stuffed Burgers with
Grilled Nectarines 35

Classic Beef Burgers 36

Brie-Stuffed Burgers with Sage Onions
on Foccacia 37

BLAT Burgers 38

Breakfast Burgers 41

Teriyaki Sliders with Grilled Pineapple 42

Pork Banh Mi Burgers with Pickled
Vegetables & Eggs 45

Spiced Lamb Sliders with Romesco
Sauce 46

Lamb & Feta Burgers with
Sumac-Yogurt Sauce 50

Buffalo Burgers with Pimento Cheese
& Bacon 51

Turkey Burgers with Cheddar,
Sautéed Onions & Bacon 53

Green Chile Avocado Turkey
Cheeseburgers 54

Chicken Burgers with Bourbon
BBQ Sauce & Mushrooms 57

Meatball Sliders with Provolone
& Peperoncini 58

Open-Face Chicken & Spinach Burgers 59

SEAFOOD
Shrimp Burgers with Herbed Aioli
& Frisée Salad 63

Shrimp Po'Boy Sliders with
Rémoulade 64

Crab Burgers with Smashed Avocado 66

Salmon Burgers with Green Goddess
Dressing & Watercress 67

Saigon Salmon Burgers with
Carrot-Daikon Slaw 69

Tuna Burgers Pan Bagnat 72

Cod Burgers with Tartar Sauce
& Lemony Slaw 74

Scallop Burgers with Lemony
Butter-Caper Sauce 75

VEGETARIAN
Black Bean Bruschetta Burgers 78

Carrot-Farro Burgers with
Curry Aioli 81

Artichoke-Spinach Burgers with
Tomato-Feta Topping 82

Mushroom-Lentil Burgers with
Gruyère & Arugula 84

Falafel Burgers with Tahini-Cilantro
Sauce 85

Sweet Corn & Red Pepper Fritter
Burgers 88

Portobello Burgers with Herbed Chèvre
& Grilled Onions 91

Eggplant Burgers with
Tomato-Ginger Jam 92

Samosa Burgers with Spicy Mango
Salsa 93

Miso Tofu Burgers with Sautéed Chard
& Asian Mayonnaise 94

Quinoa Burgers with Roasted Vegetables
& Garlic Aioli 96

Zucchini & Ricotta Burgers with
Herbed Aioli 97

SIDES & SALADS
Bistro Fries 100

Tempura Onion Rings 103

Salt & Vinegar Wedge Fries 104

Sweet Potato Fries 105

Baby Arugula & Herb Salad with
Grilled Figs & Halloumi 108

Israeli Couscous with Kale
& Butternut Squash 110

Grilled Vegetable Skewers with
Parmesan Dusting 111

Bibb Lettuce Salad with Grilled Peaches
& Prosciutto 113

Creamy Fingerling Potato Salad with
Tarragon 114

Little Gems with Blue Cheese Dressing
& Tiny Croutons 115

Fennel, Apple & Toasted Walnut Slaw 116

Chopped Salad with Grilled Corn
& Cotija 119

MENUS 122

INDEX 125

BURGERS FOR DINNER

As every home cook knows, one surefire way to elicit smiles, cheers, and sometimes even squeals of excitement from family and friends is to proclaim, "It's burger night!" It's an announcement that makes everyone stop grumbling and get into a festive Saturday-night spirit—even if it's only a weekday.

It's not hard to find a place to eat burgers. They populate the menus of both homey diners and high-end restaurants. Indeed, burgers belong to a special class of dishes—like roast chicken and Caesar salad—that often serve as an eatery's litmus test. They can be poorly executed and cast doubt on an entire operation. Or they can be done well and be the reason to return to that restaurant again and again. The modest burger holds its own against far more complicated dishes and, when made correctly, can outshine them all.

Part of the genius of the burger is the endless variety of protein and flavor possibilities. You can make burgers out of turkey, lamb, tuna, or shrimp. If it's meatless Monday, the chapter on vegetarian burgers will open up a whole range of new ideas—burgers made of carrots and farro, mushroom-lentil burgers, even an artichoke burger. Come Sunday, top that burger with some bacon and an egg and—voilà!—you've got brunch.

Burgers are a tried-and-true weeknight staple. But their versatile nature also makes them terrific for entertaining. They freeze beautifully, so you can make a big batch in advance and pull them out as needed. In these pages, you'll find a burger to suit any mood or taste. You can heap mushrooms and onions on them, top them with a salsa of grilled fruit, or slather them with your own take on "secret sauce." You can use them to showcase homemade condiments, or miniaturize them and slip them into slider buns for feeding a crowd.

Accompaniments are another wild card for the clever cook. The faithful burger not only pairs well with such traditional sides as fries and onion rings but also with healthful green salads and corn salads, with wintry slaws and summery grilled vegetables. Or move beyond your basic bun or kaiser roll and serve your burgers over rice or quinoa.

Burgers have earned their place in the kitchen pantheon. Luckily, they are simple to make, so that anyone can master them. And when you cook them at home, you can control all the ingredients and variables, which means that every burger you serve can be both delicious and a crowd-pleaser.

ANATOMY OF A BURGER

From the patty to the bun, the toppings, and the condiments, each element of a burger has an important role to play. The patty leads the charge, the toppings add flavor and texture, the condiments help marry all the ingredients together, and the bun packages everything into a satisfying meal that requires only two hands and a napkin. Follow these tips to build your perfect burger.

THE BUN

From the classic sesame bun or potato roll to more original choices like pita bread, focaccia, or baguette, your range of options is greater than you may think—as you will see in the pages that follow. Ideally, you want an equal bun-to-burger ratio. Every bite should include some of each, and the bun should never be thicker than the burger.

THE PATTY

The soul of a burger is the patty. Buy top-quality ingredients and match the seasoning to the protein so that the flavor of the patty shines through. For example, lamb patties can stand up to ground cumin and coriander, while the subtle nature of tuna calls for fresh herbs. Form the patties loosely, making them about 1 inch (2.5 cm) thick and with an indentation in the center to help them keep their shape as they cook. Make them as wide as or a little wider than the bun.

THE TOPPINGS

A fresh topping, like arugula or fennel, or pickled vegetables add pleasant contrast and crunch to a rich meaty burger. Sautéed mushrooms, caramelized onions, and other cooked toppings will boost the umami factor. Experiment with different cheeses: from mild, creamy burrata to pleasantly briny feta, nearly any type of cheese is welcome atop a burger. When you're ready to try something new, stuff the toppings inside the burger.

THE CONDIMENTS

Condiments add moisture and richness to burgers, bridging the different flavors at play. Even when time is short, consider adding a flavor twist to ordinary ketchup by mixing in salsa or Chinese barbecue sauce, or doctor jarred mayonnaise by whisking in fresh lime juice or a dash of Sriracha sauce. Pickle relish is a beloved standard, but fig jam, mango chutney, and other interesting options from the preserves aisle may win you over. To get the most from your condiments, add them between the patty and the toppings, so that they melt, spread, and drip messily.

BURGER PRIMER

Whether you are cooking on a gas or charcoal grill or in a frying pan on the stove top, here are tips and tricks to create the perfect burger—meaty and satisfying, yet never dense and bricklike. To make the best burgers, use a light touch with the meat.

DON'T FEAR THE FAT For the juiciest beef burgers, use ground chuck (80% lean/20% fat) or sirloin (85% lean/15% fat). Leaner cuts and grass-fed beef will yield a drier burger. When buying chicken or turkey, opt for dark meat. It's still lower in fat than beef and will result in a much tastier burger than white meat.

FRESH IS BEST Keep in mind that you don't need to buy ground meat. You can choose any boneless cut and then ask your butcher to grind it for you—better yet, grind it yourself. Use a coarser grind to avoid a mushy texture. For a special treat, add some freshly ground short ribs, dry-aged steak, brisket, or a combination.

EASY DOES IT When forming patties, handle the meat as little as possible to prevent heavy burgers. Use 6 to 8 ounces (185 to 250 g) meat per patty, quickly and lightly shaping it into an even disk about 1 inch (2.5 cm) thick and at least as wide as the bun. Work with cold hands and cold meat so that the fat doesn't melt.

MAKE AN IMPRESSION The edges of a burger cook faster than the center, which can cause the burger to puff up into a sphere. To avoid this, when shaping the patty, press your thumb into the center to make a dimple about the size of a quarter.

HOLD THE SALT Wait to add salt until after the patties are formed and just before cooking, and then season generously. Salt inside a patty will start to dissolve the protein strands, which will adversely affect the texture of the burger.

GRILL OR GRIDDLE? Burger lovers are divided about the best cooking method. Grilling adds terrific smoky flavor, but some insist that a griddle or frying pan allows the flavorful fat to stay with the burger during cooking. Whichever method you choose, do not press down on the meat with the spatula because it will release the juices and fat.

DON'T FLIP OUT Flip the burgers only once, and only after they have formed a nice brown seal. Don't flip too soon, and don't move the burgers around. When the burgers are ready to be flipped, they should dislodge from the cooking surface easily. If they stick, leave them to cook for a few moments longer.

COOKED TO PERFECTION The surest way to measure a burger's doneness is to check the internal temperature with an instant-read thermometer. The thickest part of a beef burger should register 130°F (54°C) for medium-rare, 140°F (60°C) for medium, and 150°F (65°C) for well-done. Let your burgers rest for a minute or two before serving to allow the internal juices to redistribute evenly through the meat.

TOOLS FOR SUCCESS

These basic tools will help you create foolproof burgers.

GRILLING TONGS & SPATULA A long-handled, heatproof pair of tongs and a spatula will make easy work of flipping and transferring food on the grill.

GRILL BASKET This tool prevents small foods from falling through grill grates.

INSTANT-READ THERMOMETER Check the doneness of burgers with this essential kitchen tool.

BAKING SHEETS A pair of rimmed baking sheets makes it easy to transport ingredients to the grill and bring cooked food to the table.

CAST-IRON FRYING PAN OR GRIDDLE Cast iron heats slowly and evenly and holds heat well, making it ideal for cooking burgers. If you like, you can even use a frying pan or griddle on the grill.

FRYING PAN SPLATTER SCREEN When cooking burgers in a frying pan, this fine-mesh screen will keep oil from spattering on the stove top.

FOOD PROCESSOR Rev it up to make quick homemade sauces, dressings, relishes, and vegetarian patty mixtures.

BRINGING IT ALL TOGETHER

Turning burgers into "burger night" is as simple as adding a few delicious flourishes. Keep them weeknight-friendly by implementing store-bought shortcuts and make-ahead tips that get dinner on the table faster. When you have more time, make a party out of it with homemade sauces, diner-style fries, and shakes.

MAKE IT A MEAL

Use these ideas as inspiration to transform burgers into unique, wholesome, and balanced meals.

BURGER SALAD Place two or three 2- to 3-ounce (60- to 90-g) slider patties on top of your favorite salad. Forgo the bun and enjoy with a fork and knife.

PUT AN EGG ON IT Top each burger with a fried egg, for a delicious and healthful way to add extra protein.

GRILLED VEGETABLES If the fire is already going, grill some extra vegetables, such as corn, zucchini, onions, or whatever is seasonally available, and serve as a topping or side dish to the burgers. In cold weather, roast the vegetables.

YESTERDAY'S BURGER Crumble leftover cooked burgers and add to scrambled eggs, salads, quesadillas, or wraps.

SHORTCUTS FOR A BUSY DAY

Most burgers come together quickly and easily over high heat, but here are some shortcuts to help put dinner on the table when time is limited and everybody is hungry.

PREP STATION For efficient burger assembly, gather together all the ingredients and tools you will need. After lighting the grill or before turning on the stove, form the patties, wash and chop the vegetables, make the sauces, and then arrange everything in a ready-to-go assembly line.

VEGETABLE TOPPINGS Save prep time by purchasing shredded and/or chopped vegetables to use as a base for a vegetarian burger mixture or as toppings.

SIDES & SALADS A mixture of lettuces dressed with olive oil and vinegar makes a simple side dish. Tuck in some frisée, watercress, or baby kale for variety. Or purchase your favorite ready-made salads from the prepared-foods section of the grocery store.

MAKE IT AHEAD

Burger night comes together in a jiffy, but here are some strategies for those really busy weeks.

FREEZE IT Both meat and vegetarian patties freeze well for up to 3 months, as do seafood patties if made from seafood that has not been previously frozen. Form the patties, stack them separated by pieces of waxed paper, and pack them into a zippered plastic bag. You will be able to remove as many patties as you need and then return the remainder to the freezer.

STOCK IT/USE IT UP Purchase sliced cheeses for ease and keep store-bought salsa and barbecue sauce on hand. For open-faced burgers, get creative with those last couple of English muffins or with day-old bread that is perfect for slicing and toasting. Similarly, leftover cooked vegetables are often good served over a burger.

PREP IT Keep washed lettuce wrapped tightly in paper towels in a zippered plastic bag. Homemade ketchup, aioli, and salad dressing will really step up your game and can be made a few days ahead. You can form the patties for every burger in this book the day before. By the time the grill is hot, your side dish will be complete, too!

WEEKEND BURGER PARTY

The weekend is a perfect time to invite over a few friends, fire up the grill, and enjoy a burger party. Keep it easy and customizable with a burger bar that allows guests to get creative with their choices.

PREP IN ADVANCE Form and refrigerate the patties a day ahead of the party. Accommodate a variety of dietary needs and cravings by making two different patties: one meat and one poultry, fish, or vegetarian.

MAKE 1–3 SIDES Turn to hearty sides that can be popped into the oven just before guests arrive and to salads that can be made a day in advance and refrigerated until serving time. See Sweet Potato Fries (page 105), Little Gems with Blue Cheese Dressing & Tiny Croutons (page 115), and Fennel, Apple & Toasted Walnut Slaw (page 116).

CREATE A BUFFET LINE Let guests assemble their own burgers: start with plates and utensils, followed by toasted buns, patties, and a variety of condiments, toppings, and side dishes. Or make the grill part of the assembly line: lay out plates, utensils, toppings, and condiments next to the grill and serve the burgers hot off the fire.

PARTY DRINKS For a diner-themed get-together, serve milkshakes in tall glasses with straws and French fries alongside the burgers. Or, go for a barbecue theme with ice-cold beers and lemonade.

ESSENTIALS

¾ lb (375 g) Kirby or English cucumbers, cut on the diagonal into ¼-inch (6-mm) slices

¼ cup (⅓ oz/10 g) loosely packed dill leaves, roughly chopped

1 cup (8 fl oz/250 ml) distilled white vinegar

2 tablespoons sugar

1 teaspoon kosher salt

½ teaspoon yellow mustard seeds

QUICK DILL PICKLES

EASY CRUNCH

→→→→→→→→→→

You'll be surprised how quickly a cucumber becomes a delectable pickle. This is a great recipe to put the kids in charge of because it's simple and fun. Kirby cucumbers are the most common for pickling as they tend to retain their crunch. You can use this same brine to pickle other vegetables such as blanched cauliflower, carrots, beets, or green beans.

Place the cucumber slices and dill into a heatproof nonreactive bowl.

In a small saucepan over low heat, bring the vinegar, sugar, salt, and mustard seeds to a low boil. Cook, stirring, until the sugar and salt dissolve. Pour the mixture over the cucumber slices and stir to combine. Let sit at room temperature until the liquid cools completely. Serve right away or store in the refrigerator in an airtight container for up to 1 week.

MAKES ABOUT 2 CUPS (10 OZ/300 G), ENOUGH TO TOP 6 BURGERS

1 can (28 oz/875 g) crushed tomatoes, with juice

½ cup (4 fl oz/125 ml) apple cider vinegar

2 tablespoons dark brown sugar

½ teaspoon onion powder

¼ teaspoon garlic powder

¼ teaspoon dry mustard

Pinch of ground cloves

Pinch of celery salt

Pinch of ground allspice

Kosher salt and freshly ground pepper

KETCHUP

BETTER FROM SCRATCH

Ketchup—an essential burger condiment—is simple to make from scratch, letting you control exactly which ingredients you want and don't want. You can freeze ketchup in batches for up to 1 month. Try dividing this recipe up, then mixing in some of the fun flavor variations on the right. They're great with Bistro Fries (page 100).

Combine the tomatoes, vingear, sugar, onion powder, garlic powder, mustard, cloves, celery salt, and allspice in a heavy-bottomed saucepan over medium-high heat. Bring to a boil and reduce the heat to low. Simmer, stirring occasionally, until the sauce reduces and is nicely thickened, about 1 hour and 15 minutes. Season with salt and pepper. Let cool completely before using. The ketchup can be stored in the refrigerator in an airtight container for up to 2 weeks.

MAKES 1¾ CUPS (14 OZ/440 G)

KETCHUP FLAVOR VARIATIONS

CHIPOTLE Add 1½ tablespoons finely chopped chipotle in adobo sauce.

SRIRACHA Add 1 tablespoon Sriracha.

SMOKED PAPRIKA Add 1 tablespoon smoked paprika.

DATE While the ketchup is cooking, substitute 5 pitted and chopped dates for the brown sugar. Let the ketchup cool, then purée in a blender until smooth.

1 cup (4 oz/125 g) ground yellow mustard
seeds

⅔ cup (5 fl oz /160 ml) apple cider vinegar or
white vinegar

1 teaspoon kosher salt

BASIC YELLOW MUSTARD

In a small saucepan combine the mustard seeds, vinegar, ⅓ cup (3 fl oz/80 ml) water, and the salt over medium heat and cook, stirring often with a wooden spoon, until thickened, about 5 minutes. Remove from the heat and let cool completely. Transfer to an airtight container and refrigerate until thickened, about 1 hour and 15 minutes. Season with salt. The mustard can be stored in the refrigerator in an airtight container for up to 1 month.

MAKES ABOUT 1½ CUPS (12 OZ/375 G)

MUSTARD FLAVOR VARIATIONS

DILL MUSTARD Stir together ½ cup (4 oz/125 g) Basic Yellow Mustard and 1 tablespoon chopped fresh dill.

HERBED MUSTARD Stir together 2 tablespoons Dijon mustard, 2 tablespoons whole-grain mustard, and 1 teaspoon *each* chopped fresh tarragon, parsley, and basil.

ROASTED GARLIC MUSTARD Roast 8 cloves of unpeeled garlic, drizzled with olive oil and loosely wrapped in aluminum foil, for 30 minutes at 450°F (230°C). Peel the garlic, mash it in a small bowl until smooth, and stir it into ½ cup (4 oz/125 g) Dijon mustard.

HONEY MUSTARD Stir together 5 tablespoons (5 oz/155 g) honey, 5 tablespoons (3 oz/90 g) Dijon mustard, and 1½ tablespoons melted butter.

HORSERADISH MUSTARD Stir together ½ cup (4 oz/125 g) Dijon mustard and 1–2 tablespoons (depending on how hot you want it) prepared horseradish.

MAKE IT HOMEMADE

It takes mere minutes to create a fresh and flavorful yellow mustard that is better than anything you can purchase at the store. To make flavored mustard, start with homemade mustard or store-bought Dijon then mix in different ingredients. Play around with fresh herbs and spice blends to create your own flavors. Mustards will keep in the refrigerator for up to 1 month.

1 clove garlic

Kosher salt

1 large egg plus 1 large egg yolk

1 cup (8 fl oz/250 ml) canola or vegetable oil

BASIC AIOLI

CONDIMENT STAPLE

>>>>>>>>>>

Both aioli and mayonnaise are burger staples, and the main difference between the two is the addition of garlic and the level of emulsion. They are readily interchangeable and both lend themselves to flavor variations. When making aioli, be sure to use a mild-flavored oil, such as canola, so that the flavor of the oil doesn't overpower the dip. Start by adding only a few drops of oil in the beginning to allow the mixture to emulsify.

Combine the garlic and a big pinch of salt in a food processor. Pulse several times until the garlic is finely chopped. Add the egg and egg yolk and pulse to combine. With the machine running, slowly drip a few drops of oil, and then follow with a slow and steady stream of oil. Season with salt and set aside at room temperature until you are ready to serve, or store in the refrigerator in an airtight container for up to 1 week.

MAKES 1¼ CUPS (10 OZ/310 G)

AIOLI OR MAYONNAISE FLAVOR VARIATIONS For each variation, stir the additional ingredients into the Basic Aioli or 1¼ cups (10 oz/310 g) mayonnaise.

MEYER LEMON Add the juice and zest of 1 Meyer lemon.

JALAPEÑO-LIME Add 2 teaspoons finely diced jalapeño chile and the juice and zest of 1 lime.

CURRY Add 1½ tablespoons curry powder and 2 tablespoons fresh lemon juice.

HERBED Add 2 tablespoons *each* chopped fresh basil and flat-leaf parsley, 2 teaspoons chopped fresh tarragon, and 3 teaspoons fresh lemon juice.

ROASTED GARLIC Omit the garlic clove in the recipe above. Roast 6 cloves unpeeled garlic, drizzled with olive oil, and loosely wrapped in aluminum foil, for 30 minutes at 450°F (230°C). Peel then mash it in a bowl until smooth. Stir into the aioli.

SPECIAL SAUCE Stir together 1 cup mayonnaise (8 oz/250 g), 3 tablespoons French salad dressing, 1½ tablespoons sweet pickle relish, 1½ teaspoons finely chopped shallots, 2 teaspoons fresh lemon juice, and season with kosher salt and freshly ground pepper.

FOR THE MILKSHAKES

1 pint (14 oz/440 g) vanilla ice cream, slightly softened

⅔ cup (5 fl oz/160 ml) whole milk

FOR THE MALTS

1 pint (14 oz/440 g) vanilla ice cream, slightly softened

⅔ cup (5 fl oz/160 ml) whole milk

¼ cup (1 ¼ oz/35 g) malted milk powder

1 teaspoon pure vanilla extract

VANILLA MILKSHAKES & MALTS

TO MAKE THE MILKSHAKES, place the ice cream and milk in a blender and purée. Serve right away in cold glasses.

TO MAKE THE MALTS, place the ice cream, milk, malted milk powder, and vanilla in a blender and purée. Serve right away in cold glasses.

MAKES 2

CLASSIC PAIRING

What could be more enticing than a burger and shake for dinner? Your kids will be thrilled with this combo anytime. The key to a great milkshake or malt is chilling the glasses in advance and adding softened ice cream to the blender. For variations, use different ice cream flavors or add chocolate syrup. A fun straw is highly recommended.

2 tablespoons olive oil

1 tablespoon unsalted butter

½ lb (250 g) white or brown mushrooms, sliced ¼ inch (6 mm) thick

¾ teaspoon kosher salt

¼ teaspoon freshly ground pepper

SAUTÉED MUSHROOMS

Warm the olive oil in a frying pan over medium-high heat and melt the butter. Add the mushrooms and stir to coat. Add the salt and pepper and sauté, stirring frequently, until the mushrooms are golden around the edges but still holding their shape, about 8 minutes. Serve right away.

MAKES ABOUT 1 CUP (6 OZ/180 G), ENOUGH TO TOP 4 BURGERS

MUSHROOM FLAVOR VARIATIONS

THYME Add ½ teaspoon chopped fresh thyme along with the salt and pepper.

LEMON-PARSLEY Add 1 teaspoon chopped fresh parsley and the zest of 1 lemon just before serving.

VERMOUTH Add 1 tablespoon dry vermouth during the last 2 minutes of cooking.

TOOTHSOME TOPPING

Simple and fast, but big on flavor and texture, sautéed mushrooms are a tasty topping to just about any burger. The trick is to gently wipe the mushrooms clean as rinsing them under water can make them soggy. Use a big frying pan so that all the mushrooms are in contact with the bottom of the pan—this will help them to caramelize rather than steam.

WHAT YOU NEED

FOR THE GRILLED ONIONS

1 yellow onion, cut into ½-inch (12-mm) slices

2 tablespoons olive oil

FOR THE CARAMELIZED ONIONS

2 tablespoons olive oil

2 yellow onions, halved and thinly sliced

1 tablespoon balsamic vinegar

FOR THE ONION-BACON SAUTÉ

4 slices thick-cut bacon

2 yellow onions, halved and cut into ¼-inch (6-mm) slices

Kosher salt and freshly ground pepper for seasoning

ONIONS THREE WAYS

VERSATILE FLAVOR

>>>>>>>>>

Of course you can always add slices of raw onion to top a burger, but cooking onions releases their sweet quality and adds depth of flavor. The trick to grilling onions is to carefully keep them in thick slices so that they don't fall apart and slide through the grates. Using a flat spatula will help hold them together when you flip them.

TO MAKE THE GRILLED ONIONS, build a medium-hot fire in a charcoal grill or preheat a gas grill to medium-high. Brush both sides of the onion slices with olive oil and season with salt and pepper. Arrange the onions on the grill grate directly over the heat and cook, turning once with a flat spatula, until nicely grill-marked, about 4 minutes per side. Transfer the onions to a cutting board and cut each slice in half, separating the individual rings. Serve right away.

TO MAKE THE CARAMELIZED ONIONS, warm the olive oil in a nonstick frying pan over high heat. Add the onions and sauté, stirring often, until translucent, about 5 minutes. Reduce the heat to medium-low and season with salt and pepper. Cook, stirring occasionally, until the onions turn deep brown, 35–45 minutes. Stir in the balsamic vinegar. The caramelized onions can be stored in the refrigerator for up to 3 days. Reheat before serving.

TO MAKE THE ONION-BACON SAUTÉ, in a frying pan over medium-high heat, fry the bacon until crispy, about 6 minutes. Transfer to paper towels to drain. When the bacon is cool enough to handle, tear it into bite-sized pieces. Set aside.

Pour off the excess grease from the pan and discard, but don't wipe the pan clean. Return the pan to medium-high heat and add the onions. Toss the onions to coat in the remaining bacon grease. Season with salt and pepper and sauté, stirring frequently, until golden, about 10 minutes. Add the bacon to the pan and cook just until warmed through, about 2 minutes. Serve right away.

MAKES ABOUT 1 CUP (6 OZ/185 G), ENOUGH TO TOP 4–6 BURGERS

BURGERS

meat & poultry • seafood • vegetarian

BALSAMIC VINAIGRETTE

1½ tablespoons balsamic vinegar

1 teaspoon Dijon mustard

Kosher salt and freshly ground pepper

1½ tablespoons olive oil, plus more for brushing

¾ lb (375 g) ground beef

¾ lb (375 g) ground pork

4 thick slices about ½ inch (12 mm) crusty Italian bread, such as Pugliese

1 clove garlic, halved lengthwise

¼ lb (125 g) burrata cheese or fresh mozzarella, drained, at room temperature

12 fresh basil leaves

1–2 ripe tomatoes, cut into 8 slices

CAPRESE BURGERS

SHOWCASE SUMMER

→⇾⇾⇾⇾⇾⇾⇾

All the fresh tastes of a caprese salad come together on this open-faced burger. If you haven't worked with burrata before, you're in for a treat; like fresh mozzarella, this Italian cheese has a firm outer skin with a creamy, tangy interior. Letting the cheese come to room temperature for at least an hour before use will ensure it's perfectly spreadable.

To make the balsamic vinaigrette, whisk together the balsamic vinegar and Dijon mustard in a small bowl. Season with salt and pepper, then whisk in the olive oil. Set aside.

Build a medium-hot fire in a charcoal grill or preheat a gas grill to medium-high.

In a large bowl, gently mix together the beef and pork. Form into 4 patties, using your fingers to create a dimple in the middle of each. Season both sides well with salt and pepper.

Brush each slice of bread with olive oil on both sides and arrange on the grill grate directly over the heat. Grill, turning once, until nicely grill-marked, about 2 minutes per side. Transfer to a work surface and rub both sides with the cut sides of the garlic clove. Set aside.

Coat the grill grate lightly with cooking spray. Arrange the burgers on the grate directly over the heat and grill, turning once, until medium, 5–6 minutes per side.

Brush the bread with the balsamic vinaigrette and spread each slice with one-quarter of the cheese. Top each with 3 basil leaves and 2 slices of tomato, brush with more of the vinaigrette, and top with a burger patty. Serve right away.

SERVES 4

1½ lb (750 g) ground beef

½ lb (250 g) cold Gorgonzola cheese, crumbled

Kosher salt and freshly ground pepper

2 nectarines, pitted and quartered

1 tablespoon olive oil

1 tablespoon balsamic vinegar

4 brioche buns, split

Mayonnaise for spreading

4 Bibb lettuce leaves

Grilled Onions (page 28) for topping, optional

GORGONZOLA-STUFFED BURGERS WITH GRILLED NECTARINES

Build a medium-hot fire in a charcoal grill or preheat a gas grill to medium-high.

Form the ground beef into 4 patties. Divide the cheese among the patties, tucking the cheese inside the meat so that it is completely enclosed. Using your fingers, create a dimple in the middle of each patty. Season both sides well with salt and pepper. Transfer to the refrigerator and let chill for 15 minutes. Alternatively, you can divide the cheese on top of the patties during the last 2 minutes of grilling, as seen in the photo.

Meanwhile, make the grilled nectarines. Brush each piece of nectarine with some of the olive oil and balsamic vinegar and season lightly with salt and pepper. Arrange the nectarines on the grill grate directly over the heat and grill, turning with tongs every couple of minutes, until soft and nicely grill-marked, about 6 minutes total. Transfer the nectarines to a cutting board and slice thinly.

Arrange the bun halves, cut side down, on the grate directly over the heat and toast until lightly browned, 1–2 minutes. Transfer to individual plates.

Coat the grill grate lightly with cooking spray. Arrange the burgers on the grate directly over the heat and grill, turning once, until medium-rare, about 4 minutes per side. Spread mayonnaise on the bottom bun, top with the lettuce, then set the burger on top. Add the nectarine slices and onions, if using, then close the burgers and serve right away.

SERVES 4

NOTCH UP THE FLAVOR

This ultra flavorful burger is a true umami sensation. Umami means "savory taste" in Japanese and is considered the fifth taste, along with sweet, sour, bitter, and salty. When selecting the nectarines, look for fruit that is ripe but not overly soft. In winter months omit the nectarines and use pears instead.

1½ lb (750g) ground beef

Kosher salt and freshly ground pepper

4 kaiser rolls, split

4 romaine lettuce leaves

1 beefsteak tomato, cut into 4 slices

Ketchup for serving

Dijon mustard for serving

CLASSIC BEEF BURGERS

PERFECT EVERY TIME

A really good burger starts with high-quality beef, so always use the best meat available. Try to handle the meat as little as possible since overworking it will result in a dense texture. Be sure to season your patties generously on both sides using kosher salt and freshly ground black pepper. Once you have mastered making the perfect burger, the choices for toppings are endless.

Build a medium-hot fire in a charcoal grill or preheat a gas grill to medium-high.

Form the ground beef into 4 patties, using your fingers to create a dimple in the middle of each. Season both sides well with salt and pepper.

Coat the grill grate lightly with cooking spray. Arrange the burgers on the grate directly over the heat and grill, turning once, until medium-rare, about 4 minutes per side. Transfer to a plate to rest and cover to keep warm. Arrange the rolls, cut side down, on the grate directly over the heat and toast until lightly browned, 1–2 minutes.

To serve, set the burgers on the rolls and top with the lettuce, tomato, ketchup, and mustard. Serve right away.

SERVES 4

3 tablespoons olive oil

2 yellow onions, halved and thinly sliced

Kosher salt and freshly ground pepper

1 tablespoon balsamic vinegar

8 fresh sage leaves, chopped

1½ lb (750 g) ground beef

6 oz (185 g) cold Brie cheese, rind removed, cut into ½-inch (12-mm) pieces

4 pieces focaccia, each about 4½-inch (11.5-cm) square

Mayonnaise for spreading (optional)

4 Bibb lettuce leaves

BRIE-STUFFED BURGERS WITH SAGE ONIONS ON FOCACCIA

To make the sage onions, warm 2 tablespoons of the olive oil in a nonstick frying pan over high heat. Add the onions and sauté, stirring occasionally, until translucent, about 8 minutes. Reduce the heat to medium-low and season well with salt and pepper. Cook slowly, stirring occasionally, until the onions turn deep brown, 35–45 minutes. Add the vinegar and the sage and stir until the liquid is completely absorbed, about 2 minutes. Remove from the heat and set aside.

Build a medium-hot fire in a charcoal grill or preheat a gas grill to medium-high.

Form the ground beef into 4 patties. Divide the cheese among the patties, tucking it inside the meat so that it is completely enclosed. Using your fingers, create a dimple in the middle of each patty. Season both sides well with salt and pepper. Transfer to the refrigerator and let chill for 15 minutes.

Coat the grill grate lightly with cooking spray. Arrange the burgers on the grate directly over the heat and grill, turning once, until medium-rare, about 4 minutes per side. Transfer to a plate and cover to keep warm.

Slice each square of focaccia open horizontally. Brush the cut sides with the remaining 1 tablespoon olive oil and place on the grill grate directly over the heat. Grill just until warmed and lightly grill-marked, 1–2 minutes.

Spread mayonnaise, if using, on the bottom halves of focaccia and top each with a lettuce leaf, a burger, a generous helping of the onions, and the top half of focaccia. Serve right away.

SERVES 4

FIT FOR COMPANY

These indulgent burgers are an excellent way to elevate your backyard barbecue. Caramelized onions take some time—although most of the cooking time is hands-off—so throw an extra onion into the frying pan and you'll have extra to use throughout the week. Tuck the onions into sandwiches, fold them into an omelet, or spoon them over grilled pork chops.

6 slices thick-cut bacon, halved

1½ lb (750 g) ground beef

Kosher salt and freshly ground pepper

1 French baguette or 8 slices toasted
sourdough bread

Meyer Lemon Aioli (page 24)

1 avocado, pitted and sliced

1 ripe tomato, cut into thin slices

4 large pieces of green-leaf lettuce

BLAT BURGERS

AWESOME AVOCADO

→→→→→→→→

Here, luscious and creamy
avocado gives this favorite
combination a new lift. For the
best results, use the very best-
quality ingredients at the height
of the season. A large lettuce
leaf makes a great gluten-free
alternative to a baguette. Select
1 large leaf for each burger then
tear the lettuce in half. Top one
half with the burger, avocado,
bacon, and tomatoes. Use the
remaining lettuce to close
the burger.

Build a medium-hot fire in a charcoal grill or preheat a gas grill to medium-high.

In a frying pan over medium-high heat, fry the bacon until crispy, about 6 minutes.
Transfer to paper towels to drain. Set aside.

Form the ground beef into 4 rectangular patties. Season both sides well with salt
and pepper. Coat the grill grate lightly with cooking spray. Arrange the burgers on
the grate directly over the heat and grill, turning once, until medium-rare, about
4 minutes per side.

Slice the baguette into 4½-inch (11.5-cm) lengths and split. Slather the cut sides of the
baguette with aioli. Top the bottom half of the bread with lettuce, then the burgers,
then layer with avocado, bacon, and tomatoes, dividing them evenly. Close the
burgers and serve right away.

SERVES 4

1 lb (500 g) ground pork

2 teaspoons fennel seeds

2 tablespoons maple syrup

Kosher salt and freshly ground pepper

4 slices thick-cut bacon

¼ lb (125 g) Cheddar cheese, thinly sliced

1 tablespoon butter

4 large eggs

4 English muffins, toasted

Meyer Lemon Aioli (page 24), optional

BREAKFAST BURGERS

In a bowl, combine the pork with the fennel seeds and maple syrup and season generously with salt and pepper. Form into 4 patties, using your fingers to create a dimple in the middle of each.

In a frying pan over medium-high heat, fry the bacon until crispy, about 6 minutes. Transfer to paper towels to drain. When the bacon is cool enough to handle, tear it into large pieces. Set aside.

Pour off the grease from the pan and discard, but don't wipe the pan clean. Return the frying pan to medium-high heat and add the burgers. Cook, turning once, until medium, about 6 minutes per side. During the last 2 minutes of cooking, top the burgers with the cheese and cover the pan to allow the cheese to melt.

While the burgers are cooking, warm the butter in a clean, nonstick frying pan over medium heat. Fry the eggs until set but still runny, 5–6 minutes.

Spread the cut sides of the English muffins with aioli, if using. Set the burgers on the muffins and top with the bacon and fried eggs. Close the burgers and serve right away.

SERVES 4

VERSATILE SPECIAL

Here's a new twist on your "breakfast for dinner" routine. Ground pork becomes extra flavorful with the addition of fennel seeds and a touch of maple syrup. You can also form the meat mixture into mini patties for a terrific addition to a Sunday brunch menu, or skip the English muffins and serve over sautéed spinach or kale.

1 teaspoon vegetable or canola oil

1 clove garlic, minced

1-inch (2.5-cm) piece of fresh ginger, peeled and minced

½ cup (4 fl oz/125 ml) low-sodium soy sauce

¼ cup (2 oz/60 g) dark brown sugar, firmly packed

1 tablespoon rice vinegar

1 tablespoon cornstarch

1 lb (500 g) ground pork

2 tablespoons chopped fresh cilantro leaves

Kosher salt and freshly ground pepper

10 Hawaiian sweet rolls, split

3 rings (½ inch/12 mm thick) fresh pineapple

TERIYAKI SLIDERS WITH GRILLED PINEAPPLE

HAWAIIAN-STYLE BURGERS

These kid-friendly sliders strike the perfect balance between sweet and savory—and each burger is just the right size for little hands to hold. To make these even more festive, look for frilly toothpicks to keep each slider closed. Serve with Sweet Potato Fries (page 105) and a salad of little gems with blue cheese dressing (page 115).

Warm the vegetable oil in a small saucepan over medium heat. Add the garlic and ginger and cook just until soft but not browned, about 30 seconds. Add the soy sauce, brown sugar, and vinegar and stir to combine. In a small bowl, stir together ¼ cup (2 fl oz/60 ml) water and the cornstarch and add to the saucepan. Bring the sauce to a boil, then reduce the heat to medium and let simmer until thickened, 3–4 minutes. Set the teriyaki sauce aside.

Build a medium-hot fire in a charcoal grill or preheat a gas grill to medium-high.

In a bowl, combine the ground pork with 2 tablespoons of the cooled teriyaki sauce and the cilantro. Season well with salt and pepper. Form into 10 patties, using your fingers to create a small dimple in each.

Coat the grill grate lightly with cooking spray. Arrange the burgers on the grate directly over the heat and grill, turning once, until medium, about 5 minutes per side. Transfer to a plate and cover to keep warm. Arrange the rolls, cut side down, on the grate directly over the heat and toast until lightly grill-marked. Transfer to a plate.

Brush the pineapple slices with teriyaki sauce and arrange on the grill grate directly over the heat. Grill, turning once and basting with more teriyaki sauce, until soft and nicely grill-marked, about 3 minutes per side. Transfer the pineapple to a cutting board and cut each slice into quarters.

Slather the rolls with teriyaki sauce. Set the burgers on the rolls and top with the pineapple. Close the burgers and serve right away.

SERVES 4–6

1 carrot, shredded

½ small red onion, halved and thinly sliced

3½ teaspoons sugar

Kosher salt and freshly ground pepper

¼ cup (2 fl oz/60 ml) rice vinegar

½ cup (4 fl oz/125 ml) mayonnaise

2½ tablespoons Sriracha

1½ tablespoons fresh lemon juice

1 lb (500 g) ground pork

4 fresh basil leaves, chopped

2 green onions, white and tender green parts only, finely chopped

1 tablespoon plus 1 teaspoon fish sauce

4 teaspoons vegetable or canola oil

4 large eggs

½ cup (¾ oz/20 g) fresh cilantro leaves

1 loaf French baguette

PORK BANH MI BURGERS WITH PICKLED VEGETABLES & EGGS

In a nonreactive bowl, combine the carrot and red onion. Add 1½ teaspoons of the sugar, ½ teaspoon of salt, the vinegar, and 3 tablespoons water and stir to combine. Let stand at room temperature.

In a small bowl, stir together the mayonnaise, Sriracha, and lemon juice. Let stand at room temperature.

In a large bowl, combine the pork, basil, green onions, fish sauce, and the remaining 2 teaspoons sugar. Form into four rectangular patties. Season both sides well with salt and pepper. Warm 2 teaspoons of the vegetable oil in a nonstick frying pan over medium heat. Add the patties and cook, turning once, until medium, 5–6 minutes per side. Turn off the heat but keep the burgers warm in the frying pan.

In a clean nonstick frying pan over medium heat, warm the remaining 2 teaspoons of vegetable oil. Fry the eggs until set but still runny, 5–6 minutes.

While the eggs are cooking, drain the liquid from the vegetables and stir in the cilantro. Slice the baguette into 4½-inch (11.5-cm) lengths and split. Slather the cut sides of the baguette with the Sriracha mayo. Set the burgers on the baguettes and top with the pickled vegetables and fried eggs. Close the burgers and serve right away.

SERVES 4

INTERNATIONAL FAVORITE

The sugar in this recipe caramelizes the burger just a bit and the fish sauce provides authentic Vietnamese flavor. Try serving this burger with the pickled vegetables and fried egg over brown rice or quinoa for a fun burger bowl. Prep note: use a nonreactive bowl when combining an acid, in this case rice vinegar, with vegetables so the vegetables will keep their vivid color and not turn brown.

ROMESECO SAUCE

8 oz (250 g) jarred roasted red bell peppers, drained

1 ripe plum (Roma) tomato, quartered

1 slice day-old white bread, torn into pieces

⅓ cup (1½ oz/45 g) raw almonds

2 cloves garlic

1 tablespoon red wine vinegar

¼ cup (2 fl oz/60 ml) olive oil

Kosher salt and freshly ground pepper

1 lb (500 g) ground lamb

3 tablespoons chopped fresh flat-leaf parsley

2 fresh mint leaves, chopped, plus more leaves for serving

1 teaspoon *each* ground cumin and ground coriander

⅛ teaspoon ground cinnamon

10 mini pita pockets, split

SPICED LAMB SLIDERS WITH ROMESCO SAUCE

LAYER ON THE FLAVOR

—————▸▸▸▸▸▸▸▸▸

Romesco sauce is a roasted red pepper purée that is thickened with almonds. The sauce can be frozen for up to 1 month. It is also fantastic mixed into pasta dishes or dolloped into soups or stews. If you can't find mini pita pockets, buy bigger pita breads and quarter them.

To make the romesco sauce, combine the roasted peppers, tomato, bread, almonds, garlic, and vinegar in a food processor. Pulse until the mixture is uniformly finely chopped, using a spatula to scrape down the sides of the bowl as needed. With the machine running, drizzle in the olive oil and process to combine. Season with salt and pepper and set aside.

Build a medium-hot fire in a charcoal grill or preheat a gas grill to medium-high.

In a large bowl, combine the lamb, parsley, chopped mint, cumin, coriander, and cinnamon. Form into 10 patties, using your fingers to create a dimple in the middle of each. Season both sides well with salt and pepper. Coat the grill grate lightly with cooking spray. Arrange the patties on the grate directly over the heat and grill, turning once, until medium-rare, about 3 minutes per side.

Slide the patties into the pitas and fill with a mint leaf and romesco sauce. Serve right away.

SERVES 4–6

1½ lb (750 g) ground lamb

3 oz (85 g) cold crumbled feta cheese

2 tablespoons chopped fresh flat-leaf parsley

Kosher salt and freshly ground pepper

8 pieces naan, each about 4½-inch (11.5-cm) square

2 tablespoons finely chopped fresh rosemary

SUMAC-YOGURT SAUCE

1 cup plain whole milk Greek yogurt

1½ teaspoons sumac

1 clove garlic, minced

1 teaspoon olive oil, plus more for brushing

LAMB & FETA BURGERS WITH SUMAC-YOGURT SAUCE

SPICE IT UP

>>>>>>>>>

Naan, an Indian flatbread, is soft, delicious, and perfect for wrapping around a burger. It becomes even more flavorful when grilled and seasoned with fresh rosemary and salt. You can also use this recipe for naan for entertaining—it's fantastic with dips and cheeses. Sumac is a Middle Eastern spice with a lemony taste.

Build a medium-hot fire in a charcoal grill or preheat a gas grill to medium-high.

In a bowl, combine the lamb, feta, and parsley. Form into 4 patties, using your fingers to create a dimple in the middle of each. Season both sides well with salt and pepper. Transfer to the refrigerator and let chill for 15 minutes.

In another bowl, combine the yogurt, sumac, garlic, and olive oil. Season with salt. Let stand at room temperature.

Coat the grill grate lightly with cooking spray. Arrange the burgers on the grate directly over the heat and grill, turning once, until medium-rare, about 4 minutes per side. Transfer to a plate and cover to keep warm.

Coat the grill grate lightly with cooking spray again. Arrange the naan on the grate directly over the heat and grill, turning once, until just lightly toasted and warm, 1–2 minutes per side. Remove the naan from the grill and, while it is still hot, brush with olive oil and sprinkle with the rosemary and a little salt.

Place 4 pieces of naan on a serving platter and top each with a burger. Dollop each burger with some of the sumac-yogurt sauce and top with another piece of naan. Serve right away.

SERVES 4

---

4 slices thick-cut bacon, halved

1½ lb (750 g) ground bison

2 teaspoons Worcestershire sauce

1 teaspoon dry mustard

Kosher salt and freshly ground pepper

4 soft rolls, split

½ cup (6 oz/185 g) pimento cheese, at room temperature

BUFFALO BURGERS WITH PIMENTO CHEESE & BACON

In a frying pan over medium-high heat, fry the bacon until crispy, about 6 minutes. Transfer to paper towels to drain.

Build a medium-hot fire in a charcoal grill or preheat a gas grill to medium-high.

In a large bowl, combine the bison, Worcestershire sauce, mustard, 1 teaspoon salt, and ½ teaspoon pepper. Form into 4 patties, using your fingers to create a dimple in the middle of each. Season both sides well with salt and pepper. Coat the grill grate lightly with cooking spray. Arrange the burgers on the grate directly over the heat and grill, turning once, until medium-rare, 4 minutes per side.

Arrange the rolls, cut side down, on the grate directly over the heat and toast until lightly browned.

Set the burgers on the rolls and top with pimento cheese and bacon, dividing them evenly. Close the burgers and serve right away.

SERVES 4

MIX UP THE MEAT

Buffalo burgers are made from bison meat. Low in fat and cholesterol, Bison meat makes healthy yet very flavorful burgers. Look for pimento cheese, a soft orange pub cheese, in the specialty cheese section of your market. If you can't find it, combine some shredded soft Cheddar cheese with a couple tablespoons of minced pimentos and a little mayo.

1 lb (500 g) ground turkey, preferably dark meat

Kosher salt and freshly ground pepper

1 tablespoon olive oil

¼ lb (125 g) sharp Cheddar cheese, thinly sliced

4 soft rolls, split and toasted

Special Sauce (page 24)

Onion-Bacon Sauté for topping (page 28), warmed

TURKEY BURGERS WITH CHEDDAR, SAUTÉED ONIONS & BACON

Form the ground turkey into 4 patties, using your fingers to create a small dimple in each. Season both sides well with salt and pepper.

Warm the olive oil in a nonstick frying pan over medium-high heat. Add the turkey burgers and cook, turning once, until opaque throughout, about 5 minutes per side. During the last 2 minutes of cooking, top the burgers with the cheese and cover the pan to allow the cheese to melt.

Spread the rolls with the special sauce. Set the burgers on the rolls and top with the onion-bacon sauté. Close the burgers and serve right away.

SERVES 4

MOVIE-NIGHT FAVORITE

Homemade special sauce will rival any restaurant version you've tried. These loaded burgers are reminiscent of classic diner burgers and are sure to please the whole family. For a family movie night, serve a platter of mini burgers (simply make 8 smaller patties and serve on slider buns) with Bistro Fries (page 100), Vanilla Malts (page 25), and plenty of napkins.

2 poblano chiles

1½ lb (750 g) ground turkey, preferably dark meat

Kosher salt and freshly ground pepper

4 slices pepper jack cheese

4 seeded buns, split

Mayonnaise for spreading (optional)

4 green-leaf lettuce leaves

Smashed Avocado (page 66)

GREEN CHILE AVOCADO TURKEY CHEESEBURGERS

TASTY TIP

>>>>>>>>>>

This classic Southwestern burger will not disappoint. The trick with a turkey burger is to use dark meat and not overcook it—since ground turkey has very little fat it can dry out easily. To save time, use roasted green chiles from a can. Serve these burgers with Sweet Potato Fries (page 105) and a cooling dip like Meyer Lemon Aioli (page 24).

Using tongs or a large fork, hold 1 chile at a time directly over the flame of a gas burner, or place directly on the grate. Roast, turning as needed, until blistered and charred on all sides, 10–15 minutes total. (Alternatively, place the chiles under a preheated broiler, as close as possible to the heating element, and broil to char them on all sides, turning as needed). Transfer the chiles to a bowl, cover with plastic wrap or a clean kitchen towel, and set aside to steam until cooled, about 20 minutes. Once cool, peel or rub away the charred skins, then seed and slice the chiles.

Build a medium-hot fire in a charcoal grill or preheat a gas grill to medium-high.

Form the ground turkey into 4 patties, using your fingers to create a dimple in the middle of each. Season both sides well with salt and pepper. Coat the grill grate lightly with cooking spray. Arrange the burgers on the grate directly over the heat and grill, turning once, until opaque throughout, 6–7 minutes per side. During the last 2 minutes of cooking, top the burgers with the cheese.

Arrange the rolls, cut side down, on the grate directly over the heat and toast until lightly browned.

Spread the bottom bun with mayonnaise, if using, and top with a lettuce leaf. Set the burgers on the buns and top with the roasted chiles and a dollop of the avocado. Close the burgers and serve right away.

SERVES 4

BOURBON BBQ SAUCE

1 tablespoon olive oil

¼ cup (1½ oz/45 g) finely chopped yellow onion

2 cloves garlic, minced

½ cup (4 fl oz/125 ml) bourbon

1 cup (8 oz/250 g) ketchup

2 tablespoons Dijon mustard

2 tablespoons balsamic vinegar

1½ tablespoons molasses

½ teaspoon *each* kosher salt and freshly ground black pepper, plus more for seasoning

Pinch of cayenne pepper

1½ lb (750 g) ground chicken, preferably dark meat

¼ lb (125 g) Monterey Jack cheese, sliced

4 seeded buns, split

4 romaine lettuce leaves

Thyme Mushrooms for topping (page 27)

CHICKEN BURGERS WITH BOURBON BBQ SAUCE & MUSHROOMS

To make the bourbon barbecue sauce, warm the olive oil in a heavy-bottomed saucepan over medium-high heat. Add the onion and cook until soft, about 4 minutes. Add the garlic and cook just until soft, about 1 minute. Add the bourbon and cook until the liquid reduces by half. Add the ketchup, mustard, balsamic vinegar, molasses, salt, black pepper, and cayenne and bring to a boil. Reduce the heat to low and let simmer, stirring occasionally, until the sauce is nicely thickened, about 10 minutes. Set aside.

Build a medium-hot fire in a charcoal grill or preheat a gas grill to medium-high.

Form the ground chicken into 4 patties, using your fingers to create a dimple in the middle of each. Season both sides well with salt and pepper. Coat the grill grate lightly with cooking spray. Arrange the burgers on the grate directly over the heat and grill, turning once, until opaque throughout, about 8 minutes per side. During the last 2 minutes of grilling, top the burgers with the cheese.

Arrange the buns, cut side down, on the grate directly over the heat and toast until lightly browned.

Top the bottom bun with lettuce, then set the burgers on the buns. Top with the barbecue sauce and mushrooms. Close the burgers and serve right away, passing extra barbecue sauce at the table.

SERVES 4

WINNING SAUCE

A burger dripping with flavorful barbecue sauce is sure to be a welcome mess. Adjust the amount of cayenne pepper depending on how spicy you want the sauce. Freeze extra barbecue sauce for up to 3 months or use it for another dinner later in the week: toss a little with shredded rotisserie chicken, mix with shredded cheese, and stuff into tortillas to make quesadillas.

1 tablespoon olive oil

⅓ cup (2 oz/60 g) chopped yellow onion

4 cloves garlic, minced

½ teaspoon dried basil

¼ teaspoon red pepper flakes (optional)

1 can (14½ oz/455 g) chopped tomatoes, with their juices

Kosher salt and freshly ground pepper

½ lb (250 g) *each* ground beef and ground pork

¼ cup (⅓ oz/10 g) loosely packed fresh flat-leaf parsley leaves, finely chopped

1 large egg, lightly beaten

2 tablespoons freshly grated Parmesan cheese

¼ lb (125 g) provolone cheese, cut into pieces to fit on top of meatballs

12 slider buns, split

¼ cup (1 oz/40 g) sliced peperoncini, drained

MEATBALL SLIDERS WITH PROVOLONE & PEPERONCINI

THAT'S AMORE

→→→→→→→→

These burgers might be messy to eat but they're worth it and definitely kid-approved! For a variation, serve these as a meatball sub by placing 3 meatballs on an Italian hoagie roll. (You can make the meatballs and marinara sauce ahead of time and refrigerate for up to 1 week or freeze for up to 2 months.) To save time, double both recipes and stick half in the freezer for a last-minute meal.

Warm the olive oil in a heavy-bottomed saucepan over medium-high heat. Add the onion and sauté until translucent, about 5 minutes. Add half of the garlic, the dried basil, and red pepper flakes, if using, and cook just until fragrant, about 30 seconds. Add the tomatoes with their juices, season with salt and pepper, and stir to combine. Bring to a boil. Reduce the heat to low and let the sauce simmer until thickened a bit, about 20 minutes. Taste and season with salt and pepper if needed. Set aside, keeping the sauce warm in the saucepan.

Preheat the oven to 375°F (190°C). Coat a baking sheet with nonstick cooking spray and set aside.

In a large bowl, combine the ground beef, ground pork, parsley, egg, Parmesan, and the remaining half of the garlic. Season well with salt and pepper and form into 12 meatballs. Transfer the meatballs to the prepared baking sheet and bake until cooked through, 15–18 minutes. Remove from the oven, top each meatball with a slice of provolone, and place back in the oven for 1–2 more minutes to allow the cheese to melt.

Set the sliders on the buns. Top with the sauce and peperoncini slices. Close the burgers and serve right away, passing extra sauce at the table.

SERVES 4–6

5 oz (155 g) fresh spinach leaves

1½ lb (750 g) ground chicken, preferably dark meat

3 oz (90 g) smoked mozzarella cheese, shredded

Kosher salt and freshly ground pepper

4 slices sourdough bread

Honey Mustard (page 21)

1 large, ripe tomato, cut into 4 slices

OPEN-FACE CHICKEN & SPINACH BURGERS

Bring a saucepan of water to a boil over high heat. Add the spinach and cook just until wilted, about 30 seconds. Drain the spinach and spread out on a kitchen towel. Let cool completely, then wrap the kitchen towel around the spinach and wring until most of the liquid is gone. Transfer the spinach to a cutting board and finely chop.

In a large bowl, combine the ground chicken, spinach, and cheese. Form into 4 patties, using your fingers to create a dimple in each. Season both sides well with salt and pepper. Transfer to the refrigerator to chill for at least 30 minutes and up to overnight.

Build a medium-hot fire in a charcoal grill or preheat a gas grill to medium-high.

Coat the grill grate lightly with cooking spray again. Arrange the bread on the grate directly over the heat and grill, turning once, just until toasted, about 2 minutes per side. Transfer to a plate.

Coat the grill grate lightly with cooking spray again. Arrange the burgers on the grate directly over the heat and grill, turning once, until opaque throughout, about 8 minutes per side.

Spread the bread with the honey mustard and top with the tomato and burgers. Serve right away.

SERVES 4

MAKE-AHEAD TIP

Placing these burgers in the refrigerator for 30 minutes before cooking will help them hold together while grilling. For these and other burgers, make a batch of patties ahead of time then freeze them for easy weeknight meals. Form the patties and place a sheet of wax paper between each one (the wax paper will make separating the patties easier). Defrost the burgers overnight in the refrigerator by separating the patties and placing them on a plate in a single layer.

1 lb (500 g) medium shrimp, peeled and deveined

2 tablespoons chopped fresh flat-leaf parsley

2 tablespoons finely chopped shallots

1 clove garlic, minced

½ teaspoon Old Bay seasoning

½ teaspoon kosher salt

¼ teaspoon freshly ground black pepper

Big pinch of cayenne pepper

4 teaspoons olive oil

1 head frisée, chopped

1 tablespoon fresh lemon juice

4 poppy seed buns, split

Herbed Aioli (page 24)

SHRIMP BURGERS WITH HERBED AIOLI & FRISÉE SALAD

Place half of the shrimp in a food processor and pulse the machine several times until finely chopped. Transfer to a large bowl. Finely chop the other half of the shrimp and add to the bowl along with the parsley, shallots, garlic, Old Bay, salt, black pepper, and cayenne. Form into 4 patties and transfer to the refrigerator to chill for at least 30 minutes and up to overnight.

Warm 2 teaspoons of the olive oil in a nonstick frying pan over medium-high heat. Add the shrimp burgers and cook, turning once, until opaque throughout, 4–5 minutes per side. While the burgers are cooking, toss the frisée with the remaining 2 teaspoons olive oil and the lemon juice and season with salt and pepper.

Spread the cut sides of the buns with aioli. Set the burgers on the buns and top with the frisée salad. Close the burgers and serve right away.

SERVES 4

PREP TIP

By whirling half the shrimp in a food processor you can create the perfect binding texture—meaning fewer bread crumbs are needed and maximum shrimp flavor is preserved. Serve with Sweet Potato Fries (page 105) and pass extra aioli for dipping.

1 lb (500 g) medium shrimp, peeled, deveined, and cut into small dice

¼ cup (1½ oz/45 g) *each* finely chopped yellow onion and red bell pepper

3 tablespoons finely ground yellow cornmeal

2 tablespoons chopped fresh flat-leaf parsley

1 large egg, lightly beaten

½ teaspoon *each* garlic powder and onion powder

¼ teaspoon dried oregano

¼ teaspoon kosher salt

⅛ teaspoon cayenne pepper

⅛ teaspoon freshly ground black pepper

2 teaspoons olive oil

14 slider buns, split

Rémoulade (recipe below)

SHRIMP PO'BOY SLIDERS WITH RÉMOULADE

NEW ORLEANS-STYLE FARE

→≫≫≫≫≫≫≫

These shrimp burgers are also terrific served atop garlic bread. Cut 1 baguette on the diagonal into slider-sized slices. Melt 3 tablespoons salted butter in a small pan over medium heat. Add 1 minced garlic clove and cook just until soft, about 30 seconds. Remove from the heat and brush each baguette slice with the garlic butter.

In a bowl, combine the shrimp, onion, bell pepper, cornmeal, parsley, egg, garlic powder, onion powder, oregano, salt, cayenne, and black pepper. Form into 14 patties and transfer to the refrigerator to chill for at least 30 minutes and up to overnight.

Warm the olive oil a nonstick skillet over medium-high heat. Working in batches, add the patties and cook, turning once with a flat spatula, until cooked through, 3–4 minutes per side. Spread the inside of the bun tops and bottoms with a dollop of rémoulade. Set the patties on the rolls. Close the sliders and serve right away.

SERVES 4–6

RÉMOULADE To make the rémoulade, in a bowl, stir together ¾ cup (6 fl oz/180 ml) mayonnaise, 2 tablespoons whole-grain mustard, 2 tablespoons finely chopped shallots, 2 tablespoons chopped fresh flat-leaf parsley leaves, and season with kosher salt and freshly ground pepper. Add 1 tablespoon fresh lemon juice and/or hot-pepper sauce to taste depending on how spicy you want the rémoulade. The rémoulade will keep in the refrigerator in an airtight container for up to 1 week.

SMASHED AVOCADO
2 avocados, peeled and pitted

2 tablespoons fresh lime juice

2 tablespoons chopped fresh cilantro

Few shakes of hot-pepper sauce, such as Tabasco (optional)

Kosher salt and freshly ground pepper

1 lb (500 g) fresh crabmeat, picked over for shells and cartilage

¼ cup (⅓ oz/10 g) loosely packed fresh cilantro, finely chopped

¼ cup (2 fl oz/60 ml) mayonnaise

¼ cup (1 oz/30 g) panko bread crumbs

2 tablespoons finely chopped shallots

2 teaspoons olive oil

4 brioche buns, split

CRAB BURGERS WITH SMASHED AVOCADO

SOMETHING SPECIAL

>>>>>>>>>

Crabmeat is a delicate and expensive ingredient that's exquisite when formed into patties. Luckily, a little goes a long way. Don't overpower the crab mixture with too many flavors—you'll want to really taste the salty sweetness of the crabmeat itself. You can also prepare these as sliders by forming smaller patties and serving them on toasted slices of baguette with Meyer Lemon Aioli (page 24).

To make the smashed avocado, add the avocados to a bowl and, using a potato masher or a large fork, mash until mostly smooth. Stir in the lime juice, the chopped cilantro, and hot-pepper sauce, if using. Season with salt and pepper and set aside.

Add the crabmeat to a large bowl with the finely chopped cilantro, mayonnaise, bread crumbs, and shallots. Season well with salt and pepper and form into 4 burger patties.

Warm the oil in a nonstick frying pan over medium-high heat. Add the crab burgers and cook, turning once with a flat spatula, until warmed through, about 6 minutes per side.

Set the crab burgers on the buns and top generously with the smashed avocado. Close the burgers and serve right away.

SERVES 4

WHAT YOU NEED

½ lb (250 g) center-cut wild salmon fillet, pin bones and skin removed, cut into small dice

6 tablespoons (1½ oz/45 g) panko bread crumbs

2 tablespoons finely chopped shallots

1 large egg, lightly beaten

1½ teaspoons Dijon mustard

2 tablespoons chopped fresh flat-leaf parsley

Kosher salt and freshly ground pepper

3 tablespoons olive oil

2 teaspoons fresh lemon juice

2 cups (2 oz/60 g) watercress, trimmed

4 hamburger buns, split

Green Goddess Dressing for topping (recipe below)

SALMON BURGERS WITH GREEN GODDESS DRESSING & WATERCRESS

In a large bowl, combine the salmon with the bread crumbs, shallots, egg, mustard, and parsley. Season with salt and pepper and stir well to combine. Form into 4 burger patties, then transfer to the refrigerator to chill for at least 30 minutes and up to overnight.

Warm 2 teaspoons of the olive oil in a nonstick frying pan over medium-high heat. Add the salmon burgers and cook, turning once with a flat spatula, until medium, about 6 minutes per side.

While the burgers are cooking, in a large bowl stir together the remaining 1 teaspoon olive oil and the lemon juice. Add the watercress and toss to coat. Season with salt and pepper.

Set the burgers on the buns and top generously with the dressing and a mound of watercress. Close the burgers and serve right away.

SERVES 4

GREEN GODDESS DRESSING To make the dressing, in a food processor, combine 1 peeled and pitted avocado, ½ cup (4 oz/125 g) sour cream, 1 drained oil-packed anchovy fillet, 1 clove garlic, 1 chopped green onion (white and tender green parts only), 2 tablespoons chopped fresh basil, 1 tablespoon chopped fresh tarragon, 1 tablespoon fresh lemon juice, and 1 tablespoon olive oil. Process until smooth and season with salt and pepper.

MAKE IT GREEN

There are many versions of Green Goddess dressing, and this one is loaded with avocado and fresh herbs. The dressing won't keep its green color for long so don't make it more than 2 hours ahead of time. You can also toss the watercress with the dressing and serve the burgers on top for a bun-free option.

1 lb (500 g) center-cut wild salmon fillet, pin bones and skin removed, cut into small dice

6 tablespoons (1½ oz/45 g) panko bread crumbs

2 tablespoons finely chopped shallots

1 large egg, lightly beaten

1 clove garlic, minced

1½ teaspoons freshly grated ginger

1½ teaspoons finely chopped lemongrass

¼ teaspoon ground cumin

Kosher salt and freshly ground pepper

2 teaspoons canola or vegetable oil

4 kaiser rolls, split

Herbed Aioli (page 24)

Carrot-Daikon Slaw (recipe below)

SAIGON SALMON BURGERS WITH CARROT-DAIKON SLAW

In a large bowl, combine the salmon with the bread crumbs, shallots, egg, garlic, ginger, lemongrass, and cumin. Season with salt and pepper and stir until well combined. Form into 4 patties, and transfer to the refrigerator to chill for at least 30 minutes and up to overnight.

Warm the canola oil in a nonstick frying pan over medium-high heat. Add the burgers and cook, turning once with a flat spatula, until medium, about 6 minutes per side.

Spread the cut sides of the buns with aioli. Set the burgers on the buns and top generously with the slaw. Close the burgers and serve right away.

SERVES 4

CARROT-DAIKON SLAW To make the slaw, combine 2 shredded carrots and ¾ cup (5 oz/155 g) shredded daikon radish in a nonreactive bowl. Add 2 tablespoons chopped fresh basil, 1 tablespoon chopped fresh mint, and ½ small jalapeño sliced and seeded, and toss to combine. Add the juice of 1 lime, 1 teaspoon fish sauce, and ⅛ teaspoon sugar and stir well. Let stand at room temperature until ready to top the burgers. The slaw will keep in the refrigerator in an airtight container for up to 1 week.

INTERNATIONAL FLAVORS

This Vietnamese-inspired burger hits all the notes: salty, sweet, and spicy. If you can't find daikon, a mild Asian radish, use matchsticks of seedless cucumber. Serve these burgers with a light side like Israeli Couscous with Kale & Butternut Squash (page 110).

WHAT YOU NEED

1 lb (500 g) fresh ahi tuna, cut into small dice

5 tablespoons (1 oz/35 g) panko bread crumbs

2 tablespoons chopped fresh flat-leaf parsley

2 tablespoons finely chopped red onion

1 tablespoon plus 1 teaspoon Dijon mustard

Kosher salt and freshly ground pepper

½ cup (4 fl oz/125 ml) mayonnaise

1 clove garlic, minced

2–3 oil-packed anchovy fillets, minced

1 tablespoon fresh lemon juice

1 French baguette

2 teaspoons olive oil

2 hard-boiled eggs, peeled and thinly sliced

2 ripe plum (Roma) tomatoes, sliced

About 8 fresh basil leaves, torn

About 12 black Niçoise olives, pitted and halved lengthwise

TUNA BURGERS PAN BAGNAT

FRENCH-STYLE SUPPER

>>>>>>>>>>

Here's a play on a classic pan bagnat—a French baguette sandwich loaded with tuna, anchovies, olives and hard-boiled eggs. Serve with Bistro Fries (page 100) and Herbed Aioli (page 24).

In a large bowl, combine the tuna with the bread crumbs, parsley, red onion, and 1 teaspoon of the mustard and season well with salt and pepper. Form into 4 rectangular burger patties. Transfer to the refrigerator to chill for at least 30 minutes and up to overnight.

In a small bowl, stir together the mayonnaise, the remaining 1 tablespoon Dijon mustard, garlic, anchovies, and lemon juice. Season with salt and pepper and let stand at room temperature.

Slice the baguette into 3½-inch (9-cm) lengths and split.

Heat the olive oil in a nonstick frying pan over medium-high heat. Add the tuna burgers and cook, turning once with a flat spatula, until medium-rare, about 4 minutes per side.

Slather the cut sides of the baguette with the sauce. Set the burgers on the baguettes and top with the hard-boiled egg, tomato slices, some basil leaves, and the black olives. Close the burgers and serve right away.

SERVES 4

1 lb (500 g) cod fillets

¼ cup (⅓ oz/10 g) loosely packed fresh cilantro, chopped

2 tablespoons soft fresh bread crumbs

1 large egg white

Zest of 1 lemon

Kosher salt and freshly ground pepper

1 tablespoon olive oil

4 soft buns, split

TARTAR SAUCE

8 cornichons, finely diced

½ cup (4 fl oz/125 ml) mayonnaise

2 tablespoons whole-grain mustard

2 tablespoons capers, rinsed

1 tablespoon plus 1 teaspoon white wine vinegar

Lemony Slaw (recipe below)

COD BURGERS WITH TARTAR SAUCE & LEMONY SLAW

MIX IT UP

These tasty burgers can be made with any firm white fish; for the freshest flavor, buy the fish on the same day you'll be using it. You don't want to handle the fish too much during cooking since it's delicate. Place the burgers in a hot, well-oiled pan and don't touch them again until it's time to flip. And resist the urge to flatten the burgers with a spatula—this will cause them to fall apart.

Cut the cod into a few big pieces and transfer to a food processor. Pulse the machine several times until the fish is finely chopped; transfer to a large bowl. Add the cilantro, bread crumbs, egg white, and lemon zest. Season well with salt and pepper and stir just until combined. Form into 4 patties, transfer to a plate, and cover with plastic wrap. Transfer to the refrigerator to chill for at least 30 minutes and up to 4 hours.

Meanwhile, make the tartar sauce. In a small bowl, stir together the cornichons, mayonnaise, mustard, capers, and vinegar. Season with salt and pepper and set aside.

Warm the olive oil in a nonstick frying pan over medium heat. Add the cod burgers and cook, turning once, until opaque throughout, about 6 minutes per side. Set the burgers on the buns and top generously with tartar sauce and slaw. Close the burgers and serve right away.

SERVES 4

LEMONY SLAW To make the slaw, in a small bowl, toss 2½ cups (7½ oz/235 g) shredded green cabbage with 2 tablespoons fresh lemon juice and 1½ tablespoons olive oil. Season with kosher salt and freshly ground pepper. Set aside.

WHAT YOU NEED

2 tablespoons olive oil

1 shallot, minced

1 lb (500 g) scallops

3 tablespoons fresh bread crumbs

¼ cup (⅓ oz/10 g) loosely packed fresh
flat-leaf parsley, chopped

Kosher salt and freshly ground pepper

4 soft buns, split

LEMONY BUTTER-CAPER SAUCE

6 tablespoons (3 oz/90 g) butter

¼ cup (2 oz/60 g) capers, rinsed

Juice of 1 lemon

SCALLOP BURGERS WITH LEMONY BUTTER-CAPER SAUCE

Warm 1 tablespoon of the olive oil in a small nonstick frying pan over medium-high heat. Add the shallot and sauté, stirring once or twice, until translucent, about 3 minutes. Transfer to a small bowl, but do not wipe the pan clean; you will use it to make the sauce.

Place the scallops in a food processor. Pulse the machine several times, until the scallops are finely chopped (it's okay if a few larger chunks remain). Transfer to a medium bowl. Add the sautéed shallot, bread crumbs, and the parsley, and season with salt and pepper. Stir just to combine. Form into 4 patties, transfer to a plate, and cover with plastic wrap. Transfer to the refrigerator to chill for at least 30 minutes and up to 4 hours.

Warm the remaining 1 tablespoon of olive oil in a large nonstick frying pan over medium heat. Add the scallop burgers and cook, turning once, until opaque throughout, about 6 minutes per side.

While the scallop burgers are cooking, make the sauce. In the same frying pan used to sauté the shallots, melt the butter over medium-high heat, allowing it to slightly brown and bubble, about 2 minutes. Add the capers and season with pepper. Cook for about 30 seconds to let the capers warm, turn off the heat, and stir in the lemon juice.

Set the scallop burgers on the buns and top generously with the butter-caper sauce. Close the burgers and serve right away.

SERVES 4

MAXIMIZE FLAVOR

Chopping the scallops in a food processor is not only fast, but it also creates a kind of "glue" that helps them form a sturdy burger. As a result, you don't need to add much filler to help bind these burgers, so you'll really taste the fresh and delicate flavor of the scallops. Make sure to use soft buns and fresh bread crumbs (not panko) as scallops are quite tender. For another fast and inexpensive seafood burger, panfry calamari steaks and top with the butter-caper sauce.

5 ripe plum (Roma) or Campari tomatoes, seeded and chopped

6 cloves garlic, minced

2½ tablespoons olive oil

Kosher salt and freshly ground pepper

1 can (15 oz/470 g) black beans, rinsed and drained

6 tablespoons (1½ oz/45 g) panko bread crumbs

¼ cup (1½ oz/45 g) finely chopped yellow onion

1 large egg

1 teaspoon ground cumin

4 slices Monterey jack cheese

4 fresh basil leaves, chopped

4 ciabatta buns, split and toasted

BLACK BEAN BRUSCHETTA BURGERS

EASY DINNER SOLUTION

>>>>>>>>>>

Canned black beans are a must-have staple to have on hand for quick protein-rich meals. Because these burgers work best if the patties are chilled before cooking, this is a great do-ahead choice for a busy weeknight dinner. When tomatoes are out of season, top with guacamole instead. Serve these burgers with Chopped Salad with Grilled Corn & Cotija (page 119).

In a nonreactive bowl, combine the tomatoes with half of the garlic and 1½ tablespoons of the olive oil and season with salt and pepper. Toss and let stand at room temperature.

Place the beans on a plate lined with paper towels. Using paper towels, blot them dry. Transfer to a bowl and, using a potato masher or fork, smash the beans just enough so they still have some chunks. Add the bread crumbs, onion, egg, the remaining garlic, and the cumin. Season well with salt and pepper and stir to combine. Form into 4 patties and transfer to the refrigerator to chill for at least 30 minutes and up to overnight.

Warm the remaining 1 tablespoon olive oil in a nonstick frying pan over medium-high heat. Add the black bean burgers and cook, turning once, until golden brown and warmed through, about 4 minutes per side. During the last 2 minutes of cooking, top the burgers with cheese and cover the pan to allow the cheese to melt.

Just before serving, stir the basil into the tomato mixture. Set the black bean burgers on the bottom buns and top with generous helpings of the tomatoes. Close the burgers and serve right away.

SERVES 4

½ cup (3½ oz/105 g) farro

2 carrots, grated

1 clove garlic, minced

1 green onion, white and green parts, chopped

½ teaspoon ground cumin

½ teaspoon ground turmeric

2 large eggs, lightly beaten

½ cup (2½ oz/75 g) almond flour

Kosher salt and freshly ground pepper

2 teaspoons olive oil

Curry Aioli (page 24)

4 soft buns, split

4 Bibb lettuce leaves

1 ripe tomato, thinly sliced

4 thin slices red onion

CARROT-FARRO BURGERS WITH CURRY AIOLI

In a saucepan over high heat, combine the farro and 2 cups (16 fl oz/500 ml) water. Bring to a boil, then reduce the heat to low. Let simmer until the farro is tender but still has a bit of crunch, 15–18 minutes. Drain the farro and let cool completely.

In a large bowl, stir together the cooled farro, the carrots, garlic, green onion, cumin, and turmeric. Add the eggs and almond flour and season generously with salt and pepper. Form into 4 patties and transfer to the refrigerator to chill for at least 30 minutes and up to overnight.

Warm the olive oil in a nonstick frying pan over medium-high heat. Add the burgers and cook, turning once with a flat spatula, until golden brown and warmed through, about 5 minutes per side.

Spread the aioli on the cut sides of the buns. Top with a lettuce leaf. Set the burgers on the lettuce and top with the tomato and onion slices. Close the burgers and serve right away.

SERVES 4

FABULOUS FARRO

Farro, a versatile grain, adds flavor and texture to this vegetarian burger. Serve these delicious patties on soft buns or use lettuce leaves as a light and crunchy alternative. The curry aioli is also tasty served as a dip for steamed artichokes or asparagus in the spring and with boiled potatoes in the fall.

3 cups (3 oz/90 g) loosely packed baby spinach

1 can (14 oz/440 g) artichoke bottoms, rinsed and drained

½ cup (3½ oz/105 g) canned butter beans

1 clove garlic

1 tablespoon plus 2 teaspoons olive oil

1 teaspoon ground cumin

1 teaspoon lemon zest

Kosher salt and freshly ground pepper

Lemon juice for tossing

4 poppy seed or sesame buns, split

TOMATO-FETA TOPPING

2 cups (12 oz/375 g) cherry tomatoes, halved

1 tablespoon olive oil

½ cup (2½ oz/75 g) crumbled feta cheese

ARTICHOKE-SPINACH BURGERS WITH TOMATO-FETA TOPPING

FLAVOR POWER

>>>>>>>>>>

The roasted tomatoes are ready in no time and add sweetness and depth of flavor to these Mediterranean-style burgers. In a pinch, raw tomatoes work just fine, too. Substitute a few sundried tomatoes if fresh tomatoes aren't in season. For the best results, use artichoke bottoms instead of hearts as the leaves make it more challenging to bind the burgers.

Bring a saucepan of water to a boil over high heat. Add 2 cups (2 oz/60 g) of the spinach and let cook just until wilted, about 30 seconds. Drain the spinach and lay flat on paper towels to cool completely. Set aside.

Combine half of the artichoke bottoms, the butter beans, and garlic in a food processor or blender. Process to a smooth purée and transfer to a bowl. Chop the remaining artichoke bottoms into small dice and add to the bowl. When the cooked spinach is cool, wrap it in a few dry paper towels and wring out the excess moisture then chop it and add it to the bowl along with 1 tablespoon of the olive oil, the cumin, and lemon zest. Season with salt and pepper and stir to combine. Form into 4 patties and transfer to the refrigerator to chill for at least 30 minutes and up to overnight.

To make the topping, preheat the oven to 450°F (230°C). Line a baking sheet with parchment paper and pile the tomatoes on top. Drizzle with the olive oil, season well with salt and pepper, and toss to coat. Spread the tomatoes in a single layer and roast in the upper third of the oven until they just start to release their juice, about 8 minutes. Remove from the oven and set the broiler to high. Top the tomatoes with the feta and broil until the feta begins to melt and turns slightly golden brown, about 3 minutes.

Warm the remaining 2 teaspoons olive oil in a nonstick frying pan over medium-high heat. Add the burgers and cook, turning once with a flat spatula, until golden brown and warmed through, 5–6 minutes per side.

Toss the remaining spinach with some lemon juice and divide among the bottom buns. Set the burgers on the buns and top generously with the tomato-feta topping. Close the burgers and serve right away.

SERVES 4

WHAT YOU NEED

2 tablespoons plus 2 teaspoons olive oil

¾ lb (375 g) cremini or brown mushrooms, sliced

Kosher salt and freshly ground pepper

2 cloves garlic, minced

1 cup (7 oz/220 g) cooked brown lentils

½ cup (2 oz/60 g) dried fine bread crumbs

1 large egg

2 teaspoons Dijon mustard

1 teaspoon chopped fresh thyme

4 thin slices Gruyère cheese

4 poppy seed buns, split

Dijonnaise (recipe below)

1 cup (1 oz/30 g) loosely packed arugula

MUSHROOM-LENTIL BURGERS WITH GRUYÈRE & ARUGULA

MEATY MUSHROOMS

Cremini mushrooms, which are actually baby portobellos, have a deep, woodsy flavor. Here, the mushrooms are processed along with lentils to a smooth consistency to help bind the burgers. Melted Gruyère, creamy dijonnaise, and peppery greens are perfect toppers to this hearty meal.

Warm 2 tablespoons of the olive oil in a frying pan over medium-high heat. Add the mushrooms and season with salt and pepper. Sauté, stirring often, just until soft but still holding their shape, about 5 minutes. Stir in the garlic and cook just until the garlic is soft, about 1 minute. Transfer the mushrooms to a food processor along with the lentils and pulse until uniformly finely chopped, using a spatula to scrape down the sides of the bowl as needed. Transfer the mixture to a bowl and add the bread crumbs, egg, mustard, and thyme. Season with salt and pepper and stir to combine. Form into 4 burger patties and transfer to the refrigerator to chill for at least 30 minutes and up to overnight.

Warm the remaining 2 teaspoons olive oil in a clean nonstick frying pan over medium heat. Add the burgers and cook, turning once with a flat spatula, until golden brown and warmed through, 8–10 minutes per side. During the last 2 minutes of cooking, top the burgers with cheese.

Spread the cut sides of the buns with dijonnaise. Set the burgers on the buns and top with the arugula. Close the burgers and serve right away.

SERVES 4

DIJONNAISE To make the dijonnaise, stir together 3 tablespoons Dijon mustard and ½ cup (4 fl oz/125 ml) mayonnaise. The dijonnaise will keep in the refrigerator in an airtight container for up to 1 week.

1 can (15 oz/500 g) garbanzo beans, rinsed and drained

¼ cup (1½ oz/45 g) finely diced red onion

¼ cup (⅓ oz/10 g) loosely packed fresh flat-leaf parsley leaves

3 tablespoons dried fine bread crumbs

2 cloves garlic

1 large egg

1 teaspoon ground cumin

1 teaspoon ground coriander

1 teaspoon kosher salt

2 teaspoons olive oil

2 pitas, halved

4 romaine lettuce leaves, chopped

2 ripe plum (Roma) tomatoes, chopped

Tahini-Cilantro Sauce (recipe below)

FALAFEL BURGERS WITH TAHINI-CILANTRO SAUCE

Combine the garbanzo beans, red onion, parsley, bread crumbs, garlic, egg, cumin, coriander, and salt in a food processor or blender. Pulse until the mixture is mostly smooth, using a spatula to scrape down the sides of the bowl as needed. Form the mixture into 8 small patties. Set aside.

Warm the olive oil in a nonstick frying pan over medium-high heat. Add the falafel burgers and cook, turning once with a flat spatula, until golden brown and cooked through, about 3 minutes per side.

Place 2 falafel burgers into each half pita pocket and fill with lettuce, tomatoes, and a generous helping of the tahini-cilantro sauce. Serve right away.

SERVES 4

TAHINI-CILANTRO SAUCE To make the sauce, whisk together ¾ cup (6 oz/185 g) whole-milk yogurt, 2 tablespoons tahini, 2 tablespoons chopped fresh cilantro, 2 teaspoons fresh lemon juice, ½ teaspoon ground cumin, and ½ teaspoon salt until thoroughly combined. Set aside at room temperature until ready to serve or make up to 3 days in advance and store in the refrigerator in an airtight container.

MAKE IT A SALAD

These burgers are delicate and best cooked in a frying pan rather than on the grill. Keeping the patties small will also ensure success when flipping them. You can make this recipe into a burger bowl by serving the patties over a bed of romaine lettuce or even couscous, dressed with the tahini-cilantro sauce. The sauce is also delicious served with grilled meats and fish or as a salad dressing.

1½ cups (9 oz/280 g) fresh or thawed frozen corn kernels

½ cup (2½ oz/75 g) finely chopped red bell pepper

½ cup (4 fl oz/125 ml) whole milk

2 green onions, white and tender green parts only, sliced

1 large egg, lightly beaten

6 tablespoons (2 oz/60 g) all-purpose flour

2 tablespoons finely ground yellow cornmeal

1 teaspoon baking powder

1 teaspoon ground cumin

Kosher salt and freshly ground pepper

2 tablespoons butter

14 slider buns, split

Jalapeño-Lime Aioli (page 24)

2 cups (2 oz/60 g) arugula

SWEET CORN & RED PEPPER FRITTER BURGERS

HEALTHY SLIDERS

→≫≫≫≫≫≫≫

Fresh or frozen corn kernels are equally good in these hearty and flavorful burgers, making them a great year-round option. The recipe yields about 14 sliders, so plan on serving 2–4 per person. These are great served with Sweet Potato Fries (page 105).

In a bowl, combine the corn, bell pepper, milk, green onions, and egg. In another bowl, whisk together the flour, cornmeal, baking powder, cumin, ½ teaspoon salt, and ¼ teaspoon pepper. Add to the bowl with the corn and stir to combine.

Preheat the oven to 200°F (95°C). Melt 1 tablespoon of the butter in a nonstick frying pan over medium-high heat. Working in 2 batches, scoop 1½ tablespoon-sized mounds of batter into the pan and cook, turning once, until golden brown and cooked through, 2–3 minutes per side. Add the remaining 1 tablespoon butter to the pan between batches. Transfer the cooked fritters to a baking sheet and keep warm in the oven.

Spread the cut sides of the buns with the aioli. Set the fritters on the buns and top with the arugula. Close the fritters and serve right away.

SERVES 4–6

6 oz (185 g) chèvre, at room temperature (about ½ cup)

1 tablespoon heavy cream

6 fresh basil leaves, chopped

Kosher salt and freshly ground pepper

4 portobello mushrooms, caps removed, brushed clean

1 red onion, cut into ½-inch (12-mm) rings

3 tablespoons olive oil

4 soft rolls, split

1 cup (3 oz/90 g) shredded romaine lettuce

PORTOBELLO BURGERS WITH HERBED CHÈVRE & GRILLED ONIONS

In a bowl, stir together the chèvre, cream, and basil until well combined. Season with salt and pepper and set aside at room temperature.

Build a medium-hot fire in a charcoal grill or preheat a gas grill to medium-high.

Place the mushroom and onion slices on a baking sheet and brush both sides with the olive oil. Season with salt and pepper. Arrange the onions and mushrooms on the grill grate directly over the heat. Grill the onions, turning with a flat spatula to keep them together, until they are very soft and have dark grill marks, 8–10 minutes total; grill the mushrooms, turning once, until they are darkened and soft, about 4 minutes per side.

Arrange the rolls, cut side down, on the grate directly over the heat and toast until lightly browned.

Spread the rolls with the herbed chèvre. Set the mushroom burgers on the rolls and top with the onions and shredded lettuce. Close the burgers and serve right away.

SERVES 4

MEATLESS MONDAY

Because it's so meaty, a portobello mushroom makes a fantastic "burger" on its own. Herbed chèvre gives a creamy texture to the finished dish. If you are cooking on a grill and find that the mushrooms and onions are burning before they soften, turn off one set of burners and set them over indirect heat; this will give them time to cook without getting additional color on the outside.

TOMATO-GINGER JAM
2 teaspoons olive oil
1 shallot, minced
1 clove garlic, minced
1-inch (2.5-cm) piece of fresh ginger, peeled and minced
1 tablespoon apple cider vinegar
1 can (14½ oz/455 g) diced tomatoes
1½ tablespoons dark brown sugar

1 small eggplant, cut into ¾-inch (2-cm) slices
Olive oil for brushing
Kosher salt and freshly ground pepper
4 slices smoked mozzarella cheese
4 slices crusty Italian bread
4 Bibb lettuce leaves

EGGPLANT BURGERS WITH TOMATO-GINGER JAM

CHOICE CONDIMENT

This tomato-ginger jam is packed with flavor and can be made up to a week in advance and refrigerated, or frozen for up to a month. You can use either canned or fresh tomatoes. Try the jam on grilled chicken or pork tenderloin, and any leftover grilled eggplant is wonderful served with hummus in a charred corn tortilla. The smoked mozzarella makes a fantastic flavor pairing here but you can change up the melted cheese topping; Monterey jack or Gouda are both great too.

To make the jam, warm the olive oil in a nonreactive saucepan over medium-high heat. Add the shallot and cook until soft but not browned, about 3 minutes. Add the garlic and ginger and cook, stirring, just until fragrant, about 30 seconds. Add the vinegar and cook for about 1 minute. Add the tomatoes and brown sugar and stir to combine. Bring to a boil. Reduce the heat to medium-low and let simmer, stirring occasionally, until the jam thickens and darkens in color, about 20 minutes. Cool slightly, transfer to a blender, and purée. Transfer back to the saucepan and keep warm over low heat.

Build a medium-hot fire in a charcoal grill or preheat a gas grill to medium-high. Brush the eggplant with a generous amount of olive oil and season well with salt and pepper. Arrange on the grill grate directly over the heat and grill, turning once, until soft and nicely grill-marked, about 4 minutes per side. Top the eggplant with the mozzarella and grill with the lid closed so the cheese melts, about 2 minutes.

Brush the bread with olive oil. Arrange on the grate directly over the heat and grill, turning once, just until toasted and lightly grill-marked, about 2 minutes per side. Spread the bread with the jam, then top with the lettuce and eggplant. Serve right away.

SERVES 4

1 medium russet potato, peeled and small-diced

Kosher salt and freshly ground pepper

½ cup (2½ oz/75 g) almond or cashew flour

¼ cup (1 oz/30 g) thawed frozen peas

1 carrot, shredded

1 large egg

1 teaspoon lemon zest

1 teaspoon garam masala

1 clove garlic, minced

2 teaspoons olive oil

4 soft buns, split and toasted

SPICY MANGO SALSA

2 mangoes, peeled, pitted, and diced

1 red jalapeño chile, seeded, ribbed, and minced

2 tablespoons chopped fresh cilantro

1 tablespoon *each* olive oil and fresh lime juice

SAMOSA BURGERS WITH SPICY MANGO SALSA

Place the potatoes in a saucepan and cover with cold water by 2 inches (5 cm). Add 1 teaspoon salt and set over high heat. Bring to a boil and reduce the heat to low. Let the potatoes simmer until tender but still holding their shape, about 6 minutes. Drain and let cool for 10 minutes.

Transfer half of the potatoes to a bowl and smash them with a potato masher or large fork until they are mostly smooth. Add the remaining potatoes, the almond flour, peas, carrots, egg, lemon zest, garam masala, and garlic and stir gently to combine. Form into 4 burger patties and transfer to the refrigerator to chill for 30 minutes and up to overnight.

To make the salsa, combine the mangoes, jalapeño, cilantro, olive oil, and lime juice in a bowl. Season with salt and pepper and stir to combine. Set aside at room temperature.

Warm the 2 teaspoons of olive oil in a nonstick frying pan over medium-high heat. Add the burgers and cook, turning once with a flat spatula, until golden-brown and warmed through, about 5 minutes per side.

Set the samosa burgers on the buns and top with the mango salsa. Close the burgers and serve right away.

SERVES 4

INTERNATIONAL FLAIR

All the rich flavors of an Indian samosa come together in this delicious burger. Garam masala is an Indian spice blend that includes turmeric, cloves, cinnamon, cardamom, and cumin. You can also make this burger using a sweet potato or yam in place of the russet potato. If short on time, use purchased mango or apricot chutney in place of the salsa.

ASIAN MAYONNAISE

½ cup (4 fl oz/125 ml) mayonnaise

1 teaspoon sesame oil

1 tablespoon freshly chopped cilantro

2 teaspoons chopped fresh chives

1 lb (500 g) extra-firm tofu, drained

3 tablespoons low-sodium soy sauce

2 tablespoons red miso paste

1 tablespoon fresh lime juice

3 cloves garlic, minced

1 teaspoon sesame oil

1 small bunch green chard, stems removed

1 tablespoon olive oil

Kosher salt and freshly ground pepper

1 tablespoon vegetable or canola oil

6 sesame buns, split

MISO TOFU BURGERS WITH SAUTÉED CHARD & ASIAN MAYONNAISE

TOFU TIPS

Weighting tofu between plates helps remove some of the moisture so the tofu will better absorb the flavors of the marinade. Topping this burger with lightly sautéed greens such as chopped chard, bok choy, or spinach adds a colorful finish that is both delicious and nutritious. Or, add crunch by using the slaw from the Banh Mi Burger (page 45) as a topping.

To make the Asian mayonnaise, stir together the mayonnaise, sesame oil, cilantro, and chives. Season to taste with salt and pepper. Refrigerate until ready to use.

Cut the tofu horizontally into 6 equal slices. Place 3 paper towels on a plate and lay the tofu slices in a single layer. Top with 3 more paper towels and another plate. Use something heavy, such as a pot, to add weight to the top plate. Let stand for 2 minutes. Change the paper towels and repeat the process once more. This will remove excess moisture from the tofu so that it will caramelize with the marinade.

In a small bowl, whisk together the soy sauce, miso paste, lime juice, 2 cloves of the garlic, and the sesame oil. Place the tofu in a baking dish and cover with the marinade. Transfer to the refrigerator and let marinate, turning once, for at least 30 minutes and up to 2 hours.

About 15 minutes before you're ready to serve the burgers, chop the chard leaves into 1-inch (2.5-cm) pieces. Warm the olive oil in a large frying pan over medium-high heat. Add the remaining minced garlic and sauté just until soft, about 30 seconds. Add the chard and season with salt and pepper. Cook, stirring often, until just beginning to wilt, about 2 minutes. Turn off the heat but keep the chard warm in the pan.

Warm the vegetable oil over medium-high heat in a clean nonstick frying pan. Let the pan get very hot, but not to the point of smoking, and add the tofu. Cook, turning once, until browned and warmed through, about 4 minutes per side. Spread the cut sides of the buns with the Asian mayonnaise and top with the tofu and sautéed chard. Close the burgers and serve right away.

SERVES 6

1 small zucchini, cut into small dice

½ eggplant, cut into small dice

1 cup (6 oz/185 g) cherry tomatoes, halved

4 tablespoons (2 fl oz/60 ml) olive oil

Kosher salt and freshly ground pepper

2 cups (13 oz/410 g) cooked quinoa

½ cup (2 oz/60 g) dried fine bread crumbs

¼ cup (⅓ oz/10 g) loosely packed fresh basil leaves, chopped

2 large eggs, lightly beaten

1 large shallot, finely chopped

3 tablespoons freshly grated pecorino cheese

2 cloves garlic, minced

Roasted Garlic Aioli (page 24)

QUINOA BURGERS WITH ROASTED VEGETABLES & GARLIC AIOLI

PROTEIN-PACKED MEAL

>>>>>>>>>>

Quinoa is an excellent source of protein and this is a great way to pack in flavorful summer vegetables. Because this burger is so hearty, it's best served without a bun, but if you want to include bread, opt for serving this dish open-faced on a slice of toasted sourdough. Use any leftover roasted vegetables in a frittata for another meal.

Preheat the oven to 450°F (230°C). Line a baking sheet with parchment paper and pile the zucchini, eggplant, and tomatoes on top. Drizzle with 3 tablespoons of the olive oil, season well with salt and pepper, and toss to coat. Spread the vegetables in a single layer and roast in the upper third of the oven, stirring once about halfway through, until very soft and slightly caramelized, 20–25 minutes.

Meanwhile, place the quinoa in a bowl with the bread crumbs, basil, eggs, shallot, cheese, and garlic. Season well with salt and pepper and stir to combine. Form into 10–12 small patties.

Warm the remaining 1 tablespoon olive oil in a nonstick frying pan over medium heat. Add the quinoa burgers and cook, turning once, until browned and warmed through, about 4 minutes per side.

Serve the burgers topped with the roasted vegetables and a dollop of the aioli.

SERVES 4–6

2½ cups (12½ oz/390 g) shredded zucchini

6 tablespoons (3 oz/90 g) whole-milk ricotta cheese

¼ cup (1 oz/30 g) freshly grated Parmesan cheese

2 large eggs, lightly beaten

2 green onions, white and tender green parts only, thinly sliced

2 cloves garlic, minced

¼ cup (1½ oz/45 g) all-purpose flour

Kosher salt and freshly ground pepper

2 tablespoons butter

14 slider buns, split

Herbed Aioli (page 24)

ZUCCHINI & RICOTTA BURGERS WITH HERBED AIOLI

Wrap the zucchini in a clean towel. Over a sink or bowl, wring out all the excess moisture from the zucchini.

In a clean bowl, stir together the zucchini, ricotta, Parmesan, eggs, green onions, and garlic. Add the flour and season well with salt and pepper. Stir just to combine.

Preheat the oven to 200°F (95°C). Melt 1 tablespoon of the butter in a nonstick frying pan over medium-high heat. Working in 2 batches, scoop 1½ tablespoon-sized mounds of batter into the pan and cook, turning once, until golden brown and warmed through, 2–3 minutes per side. Add the remaining 1 tablespoon butter to the pan between batches. Transfer the cooked burgers to a baking sheet and keep warm in the oven.

Spread the cut sides of the buns with the aioli and set the burgers on the buns. Close the burgers and serve right away.

SERVES 4-6

VEGETARIAN DELIGHT

These sliders are a great way to get little ones to eat more vegetables. Try making them with different varieties of summer squash. These burgers and the Sweet Corn & Red Pepper Fritter Burgers (page 88) both make excellent—and colorful—summer hors d'oeuvres. Serve them with sour cream and salsa.

SIDES &
SALADS

2 russet potatoes, about 1½ lb (750 g) total, peeled and cut into ¼-inch (6-mm) matchsticks

Vegetable or canola oil for frying

Kosher salt

Ketchup (page 20) or Herbed Aioli (page 24) for serving

BISTRO FRIES

CONSISTENT CRUNCH

>>>>>>>>>

The trick to crispy french fries is to double fry them, first at a low temperature and then at a higher temperature. The initial fry cooks the potatoes, while the second one gives them their golden color and a nice outer crunch. Consider using a small pot for frying—you'll need to cook the fries in smaller batches but it will use less oil and you'll have an easier time maintaining the ideal temperature.

Place the potatoes in a bowl of cold water and set aside.

Pour oil into a heavy-bottomed pan to a depth of at least 3 inches (7.5 cm). Set over medium-high heat and bring to 300°F (150°C).

Remove the potatoes from the water and let drain on a bed of paper towels, blotting them dry with more paper towels. Working in batches, carefully transfer the potatoes to the oil. Fry for about 4 minutes. There should not be any color on the potatoes at this point. Using a slotted spoon, transfer the fries to a plate lined with paper towels. Raise the oil temperature to 375°F (190°C) and, working in batches if necessary, carefully transfer the fries to the oil for a second fry. Cook just until golden brown, about 2 minutes. Transfer the fries back to the paper towel–lined plate and, while still piping hot, sprinkle generously with salt. Serve right away with ketchup or herbed aioli.

SERVES 4-6

1 cup (5 oz/155 g) all-purpose flour, plus more for dredging

½ teaspoon kosher salt, plus more for seasoning

⅛ teaspoon cayenne pepper

¾ cup (6 fl oz/180 ml) sparkling water

1 large egg yolk

Vegetable or canola oil for frying

2 yellow onions, cut into ½-inch (12-mm) rings, rings separated

Ketchup (page 20) for serving

TEMPURA ONION RINGS

In a bowl, stir together the flour, ½ teaspoon salt, and the cayenne. In a measuring cup, stir together the sparkling water and egg yolk. Add to the flour mixture and stir just to combine (over stirring will make the batter too heavy). Put additional flour on a plate for dredging.

Pour oil into a heavy-bottomed saucepan to a depth of 2 inches (5 cm). Set over medium heat and bring to 375°F (190°C).

Using tongs, dredge the onion rings in the flour on the plate, then in the batter, allowing the excess batter to drip back into the bowl. Working in batches as needed to avoid crowding, carefully slide the onion rings into the hot oil and fry, turning once, until golden brown, about 3 minutes for each onion ring. Allow the oil to return to 375°F (190°C) in between batches. Using tongs, transfer each cooked batch to a plate lined with paper towels and while still piping hot, sprinkle generously with salt. Serve right away with ketchup.

SERVES 4-6

CHANGE IT UP

This tempura coating can be used with all kinds of vegetables including carrots, mushrooms, asparagus, peppers, and zucchini. Try these onion rings with a traditional Japanese dipping sauce. Stir together ½ cup (4 fl oz/125 ml) water and ⅛ teaspoon dashi in a small saucepan. Add 3 tablespoons *each* light soy sauce and mirin, and 1 teaspoon sugar, set over medium heat, and bring to a boil. Add 2 tablespoons bonito flakes, remove from the heat, and let sit for 15 minutes. Strain the sauce and serve at room temperature.

2 russet potatoes, about 1½ lb (750g) total, scrubbed and quartered

2 tablespoons olive oil

Kosher salt and freshly ground pepper

3 tablespoons malt vinegar, plus more for serving

Ketchup (page 20) or Aioli (page 24) for serving

SALT & VINEGAR WEDGE FRIES

ROASTED PERFECTION

Roasting on parchment paper is the best way to ensure crispy oven fries. It allows the firm edges of the potatoes to stay intact, rather than sticking to the baking sheet. Malt vinegar, made by malting barley, is the traditional seasoning for British fish and chips. If you can't find it, use white vinegar as a substitute.

Preheat the oven to 450°F (230°C).

Cut each potato quarter into 5 wedges. Pile the potatoes on a baking sheet lined with parchment paper. Drizzle with the olive oil, season well with salt and pepper, and toss to coat. Spread the potatoes in a single layer and roast in the upper third of the oven, turning once about halfway through, until golden brown on the edges and fork-tender, about 25 minutes. While the fries are still hot, carefully transfer them to a bowl. Immediately sprinkle with the vinegar and more salt. Let sit for a few minutes, then serve with the ketchup or aioli, passing more vinegar at the table.

SERVES 4

2 sweet potatoes, about 1½ lb (750 g) total, peeled and cut into ¼-inch (6-mm) matchsticks

2 tablespoons olive oil

1½ teaspoons kosher salt

Ketchup (page 20) or Aioli (page 24) for serving

SWEET POTATO FRIES

Preheat the oven to 425°F (220°C).

Pile the sweet potatoes on a baking sheet lined with parchment paper. Drizzle with the olive oil, season with 1 teaspoon of the salt, and toss to coat. Spread the sweet potatoes in a single layer and roast in the upper third of the oven, turning once about halfway through, until golden brown on the edges and fork-tender, about 20 minutes. Remove from the oven and season immediately with the remaining ½ teaspoon salt. Serve right away with the ketchup or aioli.

SERVES 4-6

VARIATIONS Once you've tossed the sweet potatoes with olive oil, try the following seasoning ideas. Cooking time is the same.

ROSEMARY Sprinkle with 1 teaspoon kosher salt and 2 teaspoons chopped fresh rosemary.

CHILI & CUMIN Sprinkle with 1 teaspoon *each* kosher salt, ground chili powder, and ground cumin.

SWEET & SPICY Sprinkle with 1 teaspoon kosher salt, 2 teaspoons light brown sugar, and ¼ teaspoon cayenne pepper.

FIVE-SPICE Sprinkle with 1 teaspoon kosher salt and 1½ teaspoons five-spice powder.

VERSATILE FRIES

You can cut the sweet potatoes into any size or shape you want. Just make sure that they're cut at a uniform size, so they'll cook evenly—and remember that the thinner they are, the crispier they will get. These fries can also be deep-fried using the same method as the Bistro Fries (page 100). Serve these fries with a flavored aioli (page 24) or ranch dressing for dipping.

8 fresh or dried figs, stemmed and cut in half lengthwise

2 tablespoons olive oil, plus more for brushing

Kosher salt and freshly ground pepper

¼ lb (125 g) halloumi cheese, sliced crosswise into ⅓-inch (9-mm) thick pieces

2 tablespoons fresh lemon juice

6 cups (6 oz/185 g) loosely packed arugula

¼ cup (¼ oz/7 g) fresh basil, roughly chopped

¼ cup (¼ oz/7 g) fresh flat-leaf parsley

BABY ARUGULA & HERB SALAD WITH GRILLED FIGS & HALLOUMI

FIT FOR ENTERTAINING

>>>>>>>>>>

Halloumi is a salty Greek cheese that stays firm when grilled. You can use either Mission or Calimyrna figs, just be sure to selects figs that are still firm for the best results. This salad makes a great choice for a family-style dinner party.

Build a medium-hot fire in a charcoal grill or preheat a gas grill to medium-high.

Brush the figs with olive oil and season lightly with salt and pepper. If using dried figs, chop the figs and set them aside. Brush the cheese with olive oil. Arrange the figs and cheese on the grate directly over the heat. Grill the figs, turning once, until softened and golden, about 2 minutes per side. Grill the cheese, turning once, until nicely grill-marked, 2–3 minutes per side. Set aside.

In a large bowl, whisk together the lemon juice and the 2 tablespoons olive oil. Season well with salt and pepper. Add the arugula, basil, and parsley to the bowl and toss to coat completely. Transfer the greens to a shallow serving platter and garnish with the grilled figs and cheese. Serve right away.

SERVES 4

2 cups (16 oz/500 g) butternut squash, cut into ½-inch (12-mm) cubes

5 tablespoons (3 fl oz/80 ml) olive oil

Kosher salt and freshly ground pepper

1½ cups (9 oz/280 g) Israeli couscous

2¼ cups (18 fl oz/560 ml) chicken or vegetable broth

¼ cup (1½ oz/45 g) chopped yellow onion

1 clove garlic, chopped

3 cups (6½ oz/200 g) loosely packed chopped kale

ISRAELI COUSCOUS WITH KALE & BUTTERNUT SQUASH

ALL YEAR LONG

Israeli couscous is a pearled pasta that's bigger than regular couscous, but you can also use the more classic Moroccan couscous or even orzo for this recipe. Cooking the couscous in broth adds loads of flavor. Vary this recipe throughout the year by substituting vegetables that are in season. Try it with tomatoes and zucchini in summer, or mushrooms and asparagus in spring.

Preheat the oven to 450°F (230°C). Pile the squash on a baking sheet lined with parchment paper. Drizzle with 2 tablespoons of the olive oil, season well with salt and pepper, and toss to coat. Spread the squash in a single layer and roast in the upper third of the oven, stirring once about halfway through, until soft and slightly caramelized, about 20 minutes. Set aside.

Warm 2 tablespoons of the olive oil in a saucepan over medium heat. Add the couscous and cook, stirring often, until toasted and light brown, about 5 minutes. Meanwhile, in a small saucepan, bring 2 cups (16 fl oz/500 ml) of the chicken broth to a boil. Once the couscous is toasted, carefully add the boiling broth and bring to a boil. Reduce the heat to low, cover, and simmer until the broth is absorbed, 10–12 minutes. Turn off the heat and leave the couscous covered.

Warm the remaining 1 tablespoon olive oil in a large nonstick frying pan over medium-high heat. Add the onion and sauté until soft, about 3 minutes. Add the garlic and sauté just until fragrant, about 30 seconds. Add the kale and stir to coat in the oil. Season with salt and pepper and sauté, stirring occasionally, until the kale just begins to wilt, 2 minutes. Add the remaining ¼ cup (2 fl oz/60 ml) chicken broth and cook until the liquid is mostly absorbed, about 2 minutes. Add the squash and couscous to the frying pan and stir to combine. Season with salt and pepper and serve right away or at room temperature.

SERVES 6

WHAT YOU NEED

2 small zucchini, halved lengthwise, then cut into ¾-inch (2-cm) half-moon shapes

2 small yellow squash, halved lengthwise, then cut into ¾-inch (2-cm) half-moon shapes

1 cup (6 oz/125 g) cherry tomatoes

3 tablespoons olive oil

1 tablespoon balsamic vinegar

Kosher salt and freshly ground pepper

10 wooden skewers, soaked in water for at least 1 hour

1 tablespoon freshly grated Parmesan cheese

1 tablespoon chopped fresh flat-leaf parsley

GRILLED VEGETABLE SKEWERS WITH PARMESAN DUSTING

In a bowl, combine the zucchini, squash, and cherry tomatoes with the olive oil and balsamic vinegar. Season well with salt and pepper and stir to combine. Let the vegetables sit at room temperature for 20 minutes, stirring occasionally.

Build a medium-hot fire in a charcoal grill or preheat a gas grill to medium-high.

Thread the vegetables onto the skewers, alternating so that each skewer has a variety. Reserve the oil and vinegar at the bottom of the bowl. Coat the grill grate lightly with cooking spray. Arrange the vegetable skewers on the grate directly over the heat and grill, turning once, until the vegetables are fork-tender, 4–5 minutes per side. Transfer the skewers to a serving platter and brush with the reserved oil and vinegar. While the vegetable skewers are still hot, sprinkle with the Parmesan cheese and scatter with the parsley. Serve right away or at room temperature.

SERVES 4–6

CROWD-FRIENDLY DISH

If you are already grilling burgers, serving vegetable kebabs is a good way to keep your kitchen clean. You can use any vegetables for this recipe but the trick is to add the Parmesan while the kebabs are still hot so the cheese has a chance to melt.

4 thin slices of prosciutto, about 1½ oz (45 g)

2 peaches, peeled, quartered, and pitted

2 tablespoons plus 2 teaspoons olive oil

Kosher salt and freshly ground pepper

1 tablespoon white balsamic vinegar

1 teaspoon Dijon mustard

6 cups (6 oz/185 g) Bibb lettuce, torn into pieces

3 oz (90 g) chèvre, at room temperature (about ¼ cup)

BIBB LETTUCE SALAD WITH GRILLED PEACHES & PROSCIUTTO

Preheat the oven to 375°F (190°C). Lay the prosciutto in a single layer on a baking sheet lined with parchment paper. Bake, rotating the tray once, until the prosciutto is crispy, about 15 minutes. Set aside and, when cool enough to handle, tear into bite-sized pieces.

Build a medium-hot fire in a charcoal grill or preheat a gas grill to high. Brush the peaches with 2 teaspoons of the olive oil and season lightly with salt and pepper. Arrange on the grate directly over the heat and grill, turning as needed, until the peaches are nicely grill-marked and soft but still hold their shape, about 6 minutes total. Transfer to a cutting board and, when cool enough to handle, slice each piece into 4 wedges.

To make the dressing, combine the vinegar and mustard in a large mixing bowl. Whisk in the remaining 2 tablespoons olive oil and season to taste with salt and pepper. Add the lettuce and toss to coat completely. Season again with salt and pepper and transfer to a shallow serving dish. Garnish with the prosciutto, peaches, and chèvre and serve right away.

SERVES 4

EASY VARIATIONS

Tender greens, like Bibb and butter lettuce, are best when dressed then tossed gently with your hands rather than tongs, which can bruise the leaves. In the winter months, substitute persimmons, pears, apples, or even dried cherries for the peaches. Toasted hazelnuts or pecans are a tasty addition.

1½ lb (750 g) fingerling potatoes, scrubbed and halved lengthwise

Kosher salt and freshly ground pepper

⅓ cup (3 fl oz/80 ml) mayonnaise

1 tablespoon Dijon mustard

1 tablespoon white wine vinegar

1 shallot, minced

¼ cup (⅓ oz/10 g) loosely packed fresh tarragon, roughly chopped

2 ribs celery, chopped

3 hard-boiled eggs, peeled and quartered

CREAMY FINGERLING POTATO SALAD WITH TARRAGON

HARD-BOILED PERFECTION

To boil eggs perfectly every time, place eggs in a heavy-bottomed pan and cover with cold water by 1 inch (2.5 cm). Set the pan over high heat and bring to a rapid boil. Once the water is boiling, cover the pan, turn off the heat, and let sit for 10 minutes. Drain the eggs and rinse under cold water.

Place the potatoes in a heavy-bottomed pan and cover with water by 2 inches (5 cm). Add 1 tablespoon salt and set over medium-high heat. Bring the water to a boil, reduce the heat to low, and cook until the potatoes are fork-tender but not falling apart, about 8 minutes. Drain the potatoes and let cool for 10 minutes.

In a large bowl, stir together the mayonnaise, mustard, vinegar, shallot, tarragon, and celery. Season with salt and pepper and add the potatoes. Toss until the potatoes are fully coated and season again with salt and pepper. Gently toss the eggs into the salad and serve right away. Alternatively, you can transfer the potato salad to a shallow dish and nestle the quartered eggs into the dish.

SERVES 4–6

3 tablespoons mayonnaise

2 tablespoons sour cream

2 tablespoons buttermilk

2 tablespoons fresh lemon juice

1 tablespoon chopped chives

Kosher salt and freshly ground pepper

½ cup (2½ oz/75 g) crumbled blue cheese

3 oz (90 g) pancetta, cut into small cubes

1 tablespoon olive oil

1 tablespoon butter

1 cup (2 oz/60 g) crusty bread, cut into ⅛-inch (3-mm) cubes

4 heads (1 lb/500 g) Little Gems, leaves separated but kept whole

LITTLE GEMS WITH BLUE CHEESE DRESSING & TINY CROUTONS

To make the dressing, in a bowl, combine the mayonnaise, sour cream, buttermilk, lemon juice, chives, ¼ teaspoon salt, and ⅛ teaspoon pepper. Add the blue cheese and stir to combine. Set aside.

In a frying pan over medium-high heat, fry the pancetta until crispy, stirring occasionally, about 10 minutes. Transfer to paper towels to drain. Set aside.

To make the croutons, warm the olive oil and butter in a nonstick frying pan over medium-high heat. Allow to get hot enough to sizzle. Add the bread cubes and toss to coat each cube completely. Season generously with salt and pepper and sauté, stirring only a few times, until the bread is toasted, about 6 minutes.

Toss the lettuce with the blue cheese dressing and garnish with the pancetta and croutons. Serve right away.

SERVES 4

UPDATED CLASSIC

This is a riff on a wedge salad, a favorite accompaniment to diner-style burgers. If you can't find little gems, use a head of romaine, chopped. The blue cheese dressing can be made up to 5 days in advance but the croutons are best served hot out of the pan. Homemade croutons are a great way to use up leftover day-old baguettes.

WHAT YOU NEED

---

2 tablespoons walnuts

2 tablespoons olive oil

2 tablespoons apple cider vinegar

⅛ teaspoon sugar

Kosher salt and freshly ground pepper

1 fennel bulb, fronds removed, cored, quartered, and thinly sliced

2 cups (6 oz/185 g) shredded green cabbage

1 small Granny Smith apple, quartered and thinly sliced

¼ cup (⅓ oz/10 g) loosely packed cilantro, roughly chopped

FENNEL, APPLE & TOASTED WALNUT SLAW

SIMPLE SLAW

Crisp coleslaw is a must for any barbecue. This simple side is really just shredded vegetables tossed with dressing—so experiment with other vegetables, such as shredded broccoli, Brussels sprouts, or red cabbage, and additions, such as dill or toasted hazelnuts, to find your perfect combination. For a delicious gluten-free dinner, serve mini burger patties on top of a bed of slaw.

Heat a dry frying pan over medium heat and add the walnuts. Toast, stirring occasionally, until darkened in color and fragrant, 2–3 minutes.

In a large bowl, stir together the olive oil, vinegar, sugar, ¼ teaspoon salt, and ⅛ teaspoon pepper. Add the fennel, cabbage, apple, and cilantro. Stir to combine. Season with salt and pepper and stir in the walnuts. Serve right away.

SERVES 4

1 red onion, cut into ½-inch (12-mm) rings

2 tablespoons olive oil

3 ears of corn, husks and silks removed

Kosher salt and freshly ground pepper

1 can (15 oz/470 g) hearts of palm, drained

4 radishes, trimmed, halved, and thinly sliced

¼ cup (⅓ oz/10 g) fresh cilantro, chopped

Zest and juice of 1 lime

½ cup (2½ oz/75 g) crumbled cotija cheese or queso fresco

CHOPPED SALAD WITH GRILLED CORN & COTIJA

Build a medium-hot fire in a charcoal grill or preheat a gas grill to medium-high.

Brush the onion slices with ½ tablespoon of the olive oil and season with salt and pepper. Coat the grill grate lightly with cooking spray. Arrange the onion slices and the corn on the grill grate directly over the heat. Grill the onion slices, turning once with a flat spatula, until soft and caramelized, 4–5 minutes per side. Grill the corn, turning every 3 minutes or so, until nicely blackened, about 12 minutes total. Transfer the onion rings and corn and to a cutting board and, when cool enough to handle, cut each onion ring into quarters and remove the kernels from the cobs. Transfer the onion and corn kernels to a bowl.

Halve the hearts of palm lengthwise, then cut into ¼-inch (6-mm) slices and add to the bowl along with the radishes, cilantro, lime zest and juice, and the remaining 1½ tablespoons olive oil. Stir to combine and season with salt and pepper. Add the cheese and toss just to incorporate.

SERVES 6

PICNIC PERFECT

Corn on the cob is a natural pairing for burgers. Here, succulent grilled corn is the star of a vegetable-focused chopped salad. You can add or substitute your favorite ingredients, such as black beans and red peppers or fresh herbs like dill or basil. Cotija is a Mexican crumbling cheese that adds a salty element to this dish.

MENUS

From busy weeknights with the kids to entertaining guests on a Saturday, planning a delicious, balanced dinner is a cinch with these menus as your guide. For tips on planning a dinner see page 12.

MEATLESS MONDAY

Skip the meat in favor of lighter, yet meaty-textured portobello burgers with savory toppings.

PORTOBELLO BURGERS WITH HERBED CHÈVRE & GRILLED ONIONS (page 91)
ISRAELI COUSCOUS WITH KALE & BUTTERNUT SQUASH (page 110)
FOR THE ADULTS Red wine
FOR THE KIDS Sparkling apple juice

RETRO NIGHT

Nothing satisfies a burger craving like a classic beef patty served with a simple salad and a luscious vanilla malt.

CLASSIC BEEF BURGERS (page 36)
LITTLE GEMS WITH BLUE CHEESE DRESSING & TINY CROUTONS (page 115)
FOR THE KIDS & ADULTS Vanilla Malts (page 25)

RECHARGE NIGHT

You'll feel fueled and revitalized with this plant-based and vitamin-rich take on burger night.

QUINOA BURGERS WITH ROASTED VEGETABLES & GARLIC AIOLI (page 96)
FENNEL, APPLE & TOASTED WALNUT SLAW (page 116)
CHILI & CUMIN SWEET POTATO FRIES (page 105)
FOR THE KIDS & ADULTS Sparkling water with citrus

SLIDER NIGHT

For the perfect family meal, set up a slider bar with mini patties and buns and a variety of toppings.

SHRIMP PO'BOY SLIDERS WITH RÉMOULADE (page 64)
MEATBALL SLIDERS WITH PROVOLONE & PEPERONCINI (page 58)
SPICED LAMB SLIDERS WITH ROMESCO SAUCE (page 46)
FOR THE ADULTS Your favorite beer
FOR THE KIDS Shirley Temples

SOUTH OF THE BORDER

Taco-friendly flavors—pimento cheese, grilled corn, and salty cotija cheese—are terrific for burgers too.

BUFFALO BURGERS WITH PIMENTO CHEESE & BACON (page 51)
CHOPPED SALAD WITH GRILLED CORN & COTIJA (page 119)
FOR THE ADULTS Margaritas
FOR THE KIDS Sparkling lemonade

MEDITERRANEAN GRILL NIGHT

Enjoy this light feast alfresco, weather permitting.

LAMB & FETA BURGERS WITH SUMAC-YOGURT SAUCE (page 50)
BABY ARUGULA & HERB SALAD WITH GRILLED FIGS & HALLOUMI (page 108)
FOR THE ADULTS White wine
FOR THE KIDS Cranberry spritzers

INDEX

A

Aioli, Basic, 24
Apple, Fennel & Toasted Walnut Slaw, 116
Artichoke-Spinach Burgers with
    Tomato-Feta Topping, 82
Arugula
    Baby Arugula & Herb Salad with
        Grilled Figs & Halloumi, 108
    Mushroom-Lentil Burgers with
        Gruyère & Arugula, 84
Asian Mayonnaise, 94
Avocados
    BLAT Burgers, 38
    Crab Burgers with Smashed Avocado, 66
    Green Chile Avocado Turkey Cheeseburgers, 54
    Green Goddess Dressing, 67

B

Baby Arugula & Herb Salad with
    Grilled Figs & Halloumi, 108
Bacon
    BLAT Burgers, 38
    Breakfast Burgers, 41
    Buffalo Burgers with Pimento Cheese
        & Bacon, 51
    Onion-Bacon Sauté, 28
    Turkey Burgers with Cheddar,
        Sautéed Onions & Bacon, 53
Balsamic Vinaigrette, 32
Basic Aioli, 24
Basic Yellow Mustard, 21
Basil
    Black Bean Bruschetta Burgers, 78
    Caprese Burgers, 32
    Tuna Burgers Pan Bagnat, 72
Beans
    Artichoke-Spinach Burgers with
        Tomato-Feta Topping, 82
    Black Bean Bruschetta Burgers, 78
    Falafel Burgers with Tahini-Cilantro Sauce, 85
Beef
    BLAT Burgers, 38
    Brie-Stuffed Burgers with
        Sage Onions on Focaccia, 37
    Caprese Burgers, 32
    Classic Beef Burgers, 36
    Gorgonzola-Stuffed Burgers with
        Grilled Nectarines, 35
    Meatball Sliders with Provolone
        & Peperoncini, 58

Bibb Lettuce Salad with Grilled Peaches
    & Prosciutto, 113
Bistro Fries, 100
Black Bean Bruschetta Burgers, 78
Bourbon BBQ Sauce & Mushrooms,
    Chicken Burgers with, 57
Breakfast Burgers, 41
Brie-Stuffed Burgers with Sage Onions
    on Focaccia, 37
Buffalo Burgers with Pimento Cheese & Bacon, 51
Burgers
    anatomy of, 8–9
    busy day shortcuts, 12
    make-ahead tips, 13
    making a meal with, 12
    primer on, 11
    tools for success, 11
    weekend burger party, 13

C

Cabbage
    Fennel, Apple & Toasted Walnut Slaw, 116
    Lemony Slaw, 74
Caprese Burgers, 32
Caramelized Onions, 28
Carrots
    Carrot-Daikon Slaw, 69
    Carrot-Farro Burgers with
        Curry Aioli, 81
    Pork Banh Mi Burgers with
        Pickled Vegetables & Eggs, 45
    Samosa Burgers with Spicy Mango Salsa, 93
Chard, Sautéed, & Asian Mayonnaise,
    Miso Tofu Burgers with, 94
Cheese
    Baby Arugula & Herb Salad with
        Grilled Figs & Halloumi, 108
    Bibb Lettuce Salad with
        Grilled Peaches & Prosciutto, 113
    Black Bean Bruschetta Burgers, 78
    Breakfast Burgers, 41
    Brie-Stuffed Burgers with Sage Onions
        on Focaccia, 37
    Buffalo Burgers with Pimento Cheese
        & Bacon, 51
    Caprese Burgers, 32
    Chicken Burgers with Bourbon BBQ Sauce
        & Mushrooms, 57
    Chopped Salad with Grilled Corn & Cotija, 119

Eggplant Burgers with Tomato-Ginger Jam, 92
Gorgonzola-Stuffed Burgers with
    Grilled Nectarines, 35
Green Chile Avocado Turkey Cheeseburgers, 54
Grilled Vegetable Skewers with
    Parmesan Dusting, 111
Lamb & Feta Burgers with
    Sumac-Yogurt Sauce, 50
Little Gems with Blue Cheese Dressing
    & Tiny Croutons, 115
Meatball Sliders with Provolone
    & Peperoncini, 58
Mushroom-Lentil Burgers with
    Gruyère & Arugula, 84
Open-Face Chicken & Spinach Burgers, 59
Portobello Burgers with Herbed Chèvre
    & Grilled Onions, 91
Tomato-Feta Topping, 82
Turkey Burgers with Cheddar,
    Sautéed Onions & Bacon, 53
Zucchini & Ricotta Burgers with
    Herbed Aioli, 97
Chicken
    Chicken Burgers with Bourbon BBQ Sauce
        & Mushrooms, 57
    Open-Face Chicken & Spinach Burgers, 59
Chili & Cumin Sweet Potato Fries, 105
Five-Spice Sweet Potato Fries, 105
Chipotle Ketchup, 20
Chopped Salad with Grilled Corn & Cotija, 119
Classic Beef Burgers, 36
Cod Burgers with Tartar Sauce & Lemony Slaw, 74
Condiments, sauces & toppings
    Asian Mayonnaise, 94
    Balsamic Vinaigrette, 32
    Basic Aioli, 24
    Basic Yellow Mustard, 21
    Carrot-Daikon Slaw, 69
    Dijonnaise, 84
    Green Goddess Dressing, 67
    Ketchup, 20
    Lemony Butter-Caper Sauce, 75
    Lemony Slaw, 74
    Onions Three Ways, 28
    Quick Dill Pickles, 18
    Rémoulade, 64
    Romesco Sauce, 46
    Sautéed Mushrooms, 27
    Spicy Mango Salsa, 93
    Sumac-Yogurt Sauce, 50

Tahini-Cilantro Sauce, 85
Tartar Sauce, 74
Tomato-Feta Topping, 82
Tomato-Ginger Jam, 92
Corn
    Chopped Salad with Grilled Corn & Cotija, 119
    Sweet Corn & Red Pepper Fritter Burgers, 88
Couscous, Israeli, with Kale
    & Butternut Squash, 110
Crab Burgers with Smashed Avocado, 66
Creamy Fingerling Potato Salad with
    Tarragon, 114
Cucumbers
    Quick Dill Pickles, 18
Curry Aioli, 24

D
Daikon-Carrot Slaw, 69
Date Ketchup, 20
Dijonnaise, 84
Dill Mustard, 21

E
Eggplant
    Eggplant Burgers with Tomato-Ginger Jam, 92
    Quinoa Burgers with Roasted Vegetables
        & Garlic Aioli, 96
Eggs
    Breakfast Burgers, 41
    Creamy Fingerling Potato Salad with
        Tarragon, 114
    Pork Banh Mi Burgers with
        Pickled Vegetables & Eggs, 45
    Tuna Burgers Pan Bagnat, 72

F
Falafel Burgers with Tahini-Cilantro Sauce, 85
Farro-Carrot Burgers with Curry Aioli, 81
Fennel, Apple & Toasted Walnut Slaw, 116
Figs, Grilled, & Halloumi, Baby Arugula
    & Herb Salad with, 108
Frisée Salad & Herbed Aioli,
    Shrimp Burgers with, 63

G
Garlic
    Roasted Garlic Aioli, 24
    Roasted Garlic Mustard, 21
Gorgonzola-Stuffed Burgers with
    Grilled Nectarines, 35
Green Chile Avocado Turkey Cheeseburgers, 54
Green Goddess Dressing, 67

Grilled Onions, 28
Grilled Vegetable Skewers with
    Parmesan Dusting, 111

H
Herbed Aioli, 24
Herbed Mustard, 21
Honey Mustard, 21
Horseradish Mustard, 21

I
Israeli Couscous with Kale
    & Butternut Squash, 110

J
Jalapeño-Lime Aioli, 24

K
Kale & Butternut Squash,
    Israeli Couscous with, 110
Ketchup, 20

L
Lamb
    Lamb & Feta Burgers with
        Sumac-Yogurt Sauce, 50
    Spiced Lamb Sliders with Romesco Sauce, 46
Lemons
    Lemon-Parsley Mushrooms, 27
    Lemony Butter-Caper Sauce, 75
    Lemony Slaw, 74
    Meyer Lemon Aioli, 24
Lentil-Mushroom Burgers with
    Gruyère & Arugula, 84
Lettuce
    Bibb Lettuce Salad with Grilled Peaches
        & Prosciutto, 113
    Little Gems with Blue Cheese Dressing
        & Tiny Croutons, 115
Lime, Jalapeño Aioli, 24

M
Malts, Vanilla, 25
Mango Salsa, Spicy, 93
Meatball Sliders with Provolone & Peperoncini, 58
Meyer Lemon Aioli, 24
Milkshakes, Vanilla, 25
Miso Tofu Burgers with Sautéed Chard
    & Asian Mayonnaise, 94
Mushrooms
    Chicken Burgers with Bourbon BBQ Sauce
        & Mushrooms, 57

Mushroom-Lentil Burgers with
    Gruyère & Arugula, 84
Portobello Burgers with Herbed Chèvre
    & Grilled Onions, 91
Sautéed Mushrooms, 27
Mustard
    Basic Yellow Mustard, 21
    Dijonnaise, 84

N
Nectarines, Grilled, Gorgonzola-Stuffed
    Burgers with, 35

O
Onions
    Brie-Stuffed Burgers with Sage Onions
        on Focaccia, 37
    Onions Three Ways, 28
    Portobello Burgers with Herbed Chèvre
        & Grilled Onions, 91
    Tempura Onion Rings, 103
    Turkey Burgers with Cheddar,
        Sautéed Onions & Bacon, 53
Open-Face Chicken & Spinach Burgers, 59

P
Peaches, Grilled, & Prosciutto, Bibb Lettuce
    Salad with, 113
Peppers
    Chipotle Ketchup, 20
    Green Chile Avocado Turkey Cheeseburgers, 54
    Meatball Sliders with Provolone
        & Peperoncini, 58
    Romesco Sauce, 46
    Sweet Corn & Red Pepper Fritter Burgers, 88
Pickles, Quick Dill, 18
Pineapple, Grilled, Teriyaki Sliders with, 42
Pork. See also Bacon
    Bibb Lettuce Salad with Grilled Peaches
        & Prosciutto, 113
    Breakfast Burgers, 41
    Caprese Burgers, 32
    Meatball Sliders with Provolone
        & Peperoncini, 58
    Pork Banh Mi Burgers with
        Pickled Vegetables & Eggs, 45
    Teriyaki Sliders with Grilled Pineapple, 42
Portobello Burgers with Herbed Chèvre
    & Grilled Onions, 91
Potatoes
    Bistro Fries, 100
    Creamy Fingerling Potato Salad with
        Tarragon, 114

Salt & Vinegar Wedge Fries, 104
Samosa Burgers with Spicy Mango Salsa, 93
Sweet Potato Fries, 105
Prosciutto & Grilled Peaches, Bibb Lettuce
   Salad with, 113

Q
Quick Dill Pickles, 18
Quinoa Burgers with Roasted Vegetables
   & Garlic Aioli, 96

R
Rémoulade, 64
Roasted Garlic Aioli, 24
Roasted Garlic Mustard, 21
Romesco Sauce, 46
Rosemary Sweet Potato Fries, 105

S
Saigon Salmon Burgers with
   Carrot-Daikon Slaw, 69
Salads. See also Slaws
   Baby Arugula & Herb Salad with
      Grilled Figs & Halloumi, 108
   Bibb Lettuce Salad with Grilled Peaches
      & Prosciutto, 113
   Chopped Salad with Grilled Corn & Cotija, 119
   Creamy Fingerling Potato Salad with
      Tarragon, 114
   Little Gems with Blue Cheese Dressing
      & Tiny Croutons, 115
Salmon
   Saigon Salmon Burgers with
      Carrot-Daikon Slaw, 69
   Salmon Burgers with Green Goddess Dressing
      & Watercress, 67
Salt & Vinegar Wedge Fries, 104
Samosa Burgers with Spicy Mango Salsa, 93
Sautéed Mushrooms, 27
Scallop Burgers with Lemony
   Butter-Caper Sauce, 75
Seafood
   Cod Burgers with Tartar Sauce
      & Lemony Slaw, 74
   Crab Burgers with Smashed Avocado, 66
   Saigon Salmon Burgers with
      Carrot-Daikon Slaw, 69
   Salmon Burgers with Green Goddess Dressing
      & Watercress, 67
   Scallop Burgers with Lemony
      Butter-Caper Sauce, 75
   Shrimp Burgers with Herbed Aioli
      & Frisée Salad, 63
   Shrimp Po'boy Sliders with Rémoulade, 64

Tuna Burgers Pan Bagnat, 72
Shrimp Burgers with Herbed Aioli
   & Frisée Salad, 63
Shrimp Po'boy Sliders with Rémoulade, 64
Sides. See also Salads
   Bistro Fries, 100
   Grilled Vegetable Skewers with
      Parmesan Dusting, 111
   Israeli Couscous with Kale
      & Butternut Squash, 110
   Salt & Vinegar Wedge Fries, 104
   Sweet Potato Fries, 105
   Tempura Onion Rings, 103
Slaws
   Carrot-Daikon Slaw, 69
   Fennel, Apple & Toasted Walnut Slaw, 116
   Lemony Slaw, 74
Smoked Paprika Ketchup, 20
Special Sauce, 24
Spiced Lamb Sliders with Romesco Sauce, 46
Spicy Mango Salsa, 93
Spinach
   Artichoke-Spinach Burgers with
      Tomato-Feta Topping, 82
   Open-Face Chicken & Spinach Burgers, 59
Squash
   Grilled Vegetable Skewers with
      Parmesan Dusting, 111
   Israeli Couscous with Kale
      & Butternut Squash, 110
   Quinoa Burgers with Roasted Vegetables
      & Garlic Aioli, 96
   Zucchini & Ricotta Burgers with
      Herbed Aioli, 97
Sriracha Ketchup, 20
Sumac-Yogurt Sauce, 50
Sweet Corn & Red Pepper Fritter Burgers, 88
Sweet Potato Fries, 105
Sweet & Spicy Sweet Potato Fries, 105

T
Tahini-Cilantro Sauce, 85
Tartar Sauce, 74
Tempura Onion Rings, 103
Teriyaki Sliders with Grilled Pineapple, 42
Thyme Mushrooms, 27
Tofu Miso Burgers with Sautéed Chard
   & Asian Mayonnaise, 94
Tomatoes
   Black Bean Bruschetta Burgers, 78
   BLAT Burgers, 38
   Caprese Burgers, 32
   Ketchup, 20
   Meatball Sliders with Provolone
      & Peperoncini, 58

Quinoa Burgers with Roasted Vegetables
   & Garlic Aioli, 96
Romesco Sauce, 46
Tomato-Feta Topping, 82
Tomato-Ginger Jam, 92
Tuna Burgers Pan Bagnat, 72
Turkey
   Green Chile Avocado Turkey
      Cheeseburgers, 54
   Turkey Burgers with Cheddar,
      Sautéed Onions & Bacon, 53

V
Vanilla Milkshakes & Malts, 25
Vegetarian burgers
   Artichoke-Spinach Burgers with
      Tomato-Feta Topping, 82
   Black Bean Bruschetta Burgers, 78
   Carrot-Farro Burgers with Curry Aioli, 81
   Eggplant Burgers with Tomato-Ginger Jam, 92
   Falafel Burgers with Tahini-Cilantro Sauce, 85
   Miso Tofu Burgers with Sautéed Chard
      & Asian Mayonnaise, 94
   Mushroom-Lentil Burgers with
      Gruyère & Arugula, 84
   Portobello Burgers with Herbed Chèvre
      & Grilled Onions, 91
   Quinoa Burgers with Roasted Vegetables
      & Garlic Aioli, 96
   Samosa Burgers with Spicy Mango Salsa, 93
   Sweet Corn & Red Pepper Fritter Burgers, 88
   Zucchini & Ricotta Burgers with
      Herbed Aioli, 97
Vermouth Mushrooms, 27

W
Watercress & Green Goddess Dressing,
   Salmon Burgers with, 67

Y
Yogurt
   Sumac-Yogurt Sauce, 50
   Tahini-Cilantro Sauce, 85

Z
Zucchini
   Grilled Vegetable Skewers with
      Parmesan Dusting, 111
   Quinoa Burgers with Roasted Vegetables
      & Garlic Aioli, 96
   Zucchini & Ricotta Burgers with
      Herbed Aioli, 97

weldonowen

1045 Sansome Street, Suite 100, San Francisco, CA 94111
www.weldonowen.com

BURGER NIGHT
Conceived and produced by Weldon Owen, Inc.
In collaboration with Williams-Sonoma, Inc.
3250 Van Ness Avenue, San Francisco, CA 94109

A WELDON OWEN PRODUCTION
Copyright © 2015 Weldon Owen, Inc.
and Williams-Sonoma, Inc.

All rights reserved, including the right of
reproduction in whole or in part in any form.

Printed and bound in China by 1010 Printing, Ltd.

First printed in 2015
10 9 8 7 6 5 4 3 2

Library of Congress Cataloging-in-Publication
data is available.

ISBN 13: 978-1-61628-734-4
ISBN 10: 1-61628-734-9

Weldon Owen is a division of
BONNIER

WELDON OWEN, INC
President & Publisher Roger Shaw
SVP, Sales & Marketing Amy Kaneko
Finance Manager Philip Paulick

Associate Publisher Amy Marr
Associate Editor Emma Rudolph

Creative Director Kelly Booth
Art Director Marisa Kwek
Senior Production Designer Rachel Lopez Metzger

Production Director Chris Hemesath
Associate Production Director Michelle Duggan

Director of Enterprise Systems Shawn Macey
Imaging Manager Don Hill

Photographer Erin Kunkel
Food Stylist Erin Quon
Prop Stylist Emma Star Jensen

ACKNOWLEDGMENTS
Weldon Owen wishes to thank the following people for their generous support in producing this book:
David Bornfriend, Elizabeth Herr, Kim Laidlaw, Elizabeth Parson, Riley Rearden, Sharon Silva, and Jane Tunks.